# Nakama 1a

INTRODUCTORY JAPANESE: *COMMUNICATION, CULTURE, CONTEXT*

## Student Activities Manual

### Second Edition

**Yukiko Abe Hatasa**
Hiroshima University

**Kazumi Hatasa**
Purdue University
The Japanese School, Middlebury College

**Noriko Hanabusa**
University of Notre Dame

HEINLE
CENGAGE Learning™

Australia • Brazil • Japan • Korea • Mexico • Singapore • Spain • United Kingdom • United States

**Nakama 1a: Student Activities Manual, Second Edition**
**Yukiko Abe Hatasa, Kazumi Hatasa, Noriko Hanabusa**

Executive Publisher: Rolando Hernández

Senior Sponsoring Editor: Glenn A. Wilson

Executive Marketing Director: Eileen Bernadette Moran

Development Editor: Kim Beuttler

Project Editor: Michael Kelsey

New Title Project Manager: Susan Peltier

Marketing Associate: Lorreen Ruth Pelletier

Illustrations: Kazuko Yokoi, Kazumi Hatasa, and Inari Information Services, Inc.



ISBN-13: 978-0-618-96570-0

ISBN-10: 0-618-96570-X

**Heinle**
25 Thomson Place
Boston, MA 02210
USA

Cengage Learning is a leading provider of customized learning solutions with office locations around the globe, including Singapore, the United Kingdom, Australia, Mexico, Brazil, and Japan. Locate your local office at **international.cengage.com/region**

Cengage Learning products are represented in Canada by Nelson Education, Ltd.

For your course and learning solutions, visit **academic.cengage.com**

Purchase any of our products at your local college store or at our preferred online store **www.ichapters.com**

Printed in the United States of America
3 4 5 6 7 11 10 09

# CONTENTS

# TO THE STUDENT

The Student Activities Manual (SAM) accompanying *Nakama 1a: Introductory Japanese: Communication, Culture, Context* is designed to increase your accuracy in grammar usage and your knowledge of **kanji**, and to help you develop basic listening comprehension and production skills in Japanese. The exercises and activities in the SAM are divided into two sections for each chapter. The workbook activities consist of vocabulary, grammar, and written exercises, and the lab activities provide pronunciation, listening, and oral production exercises. The pages have been perforated so they can be handed in. The three-hole punch design will allow you to hold onto them for reference and test preparation.

For regular chapters, the workbook section consists of the supplementary vocabulary activities followed by supplementary grammar practice to complement those in the text. The grammar activities also include a number of exercises with personalized questions that enable you to practice more creatively the central grammar principles covered in each chapter. The grammar exercises in the workbook, like those in the textbook, are situation-based and reinforce the basic vocabulary in the textbook. Following an integration section, the writing section (**kaku renshuu**) provides penmanship practice for new **kanji** and exercises that reinforce your usage of **kanji** when writing in Japanese.

The lab activities consist of vocabulary pronunciation and practice, speaking and listening comprehension activities, and a Dict-a-Conversation. In the first section, you will hear vocabulary pronounced from your textbook chapter. While listening to the audio materials, you should look at that particular chapter in your textbook, and repeat the items to familiarize yourself with the visual symbols and their sounds. Some chapters include an extra section for additional vocabulary practice. The second section provides supplementary listening and oral production exercises to complement those in the text. The exercises include formation exercises, true/false and multiple-choice exercises, task-based listening activities, and personalized questions. The last section is a dictation practice activity that will allow you to further hone both your listening and writing skills.

Name ______________________ Class ______________ Date ________________

Chapter 1

だいいっか

# The Japanese Sound System and Hiragana

## Workbook Activities

### I. Hiragana あ～そ

A. Write each **hiragana**, following the correct stroke order. The arrows indicate the direction of each stroke. Pay attention to the balance of each character and how each stroke ends: *Stop* (S), *Release* (R), or *Hook* (H). H/S indicates individual variations.

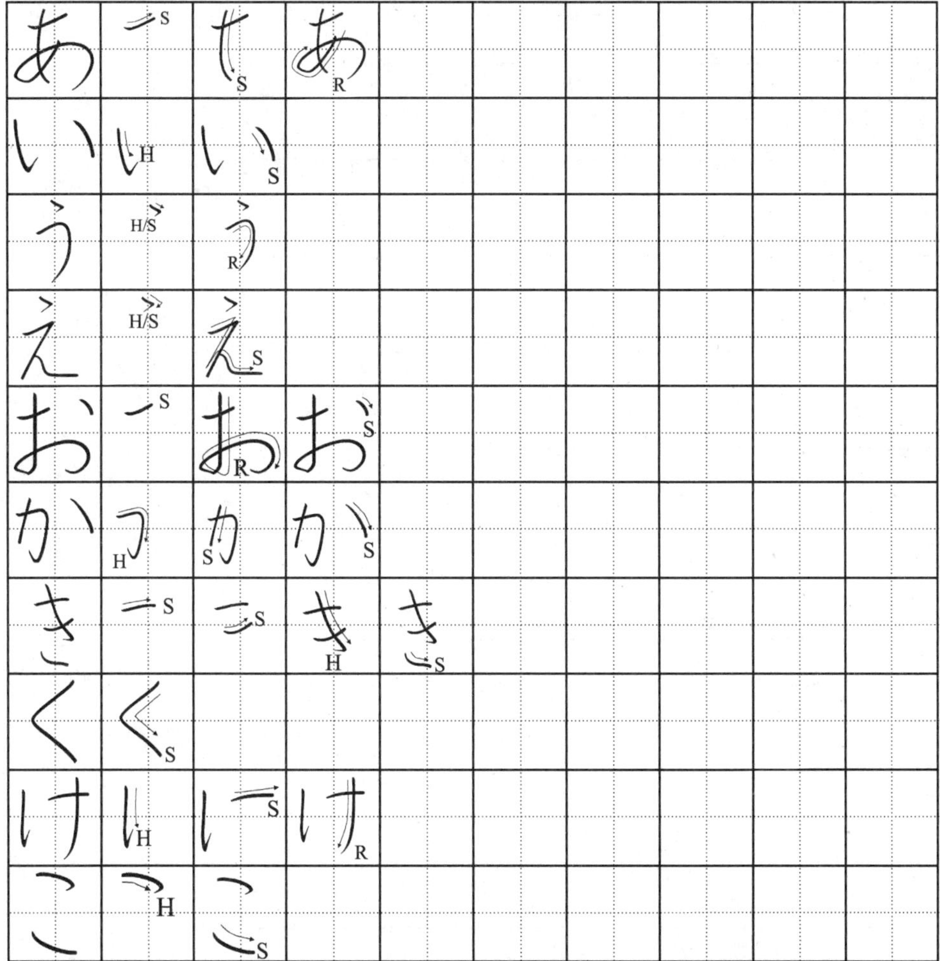

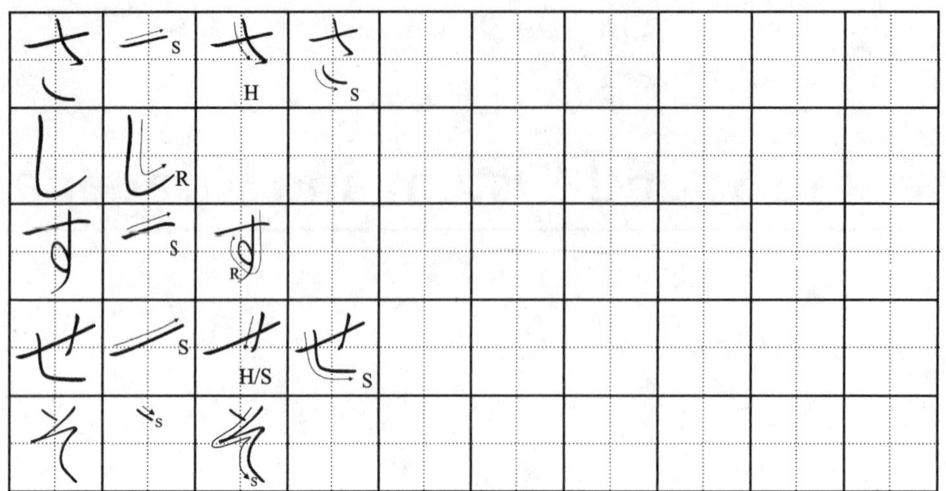


B. Practice writing each **hiragana**, following the correct stroke order. Work from top to bottom to avoid writing the same character repeatedly.

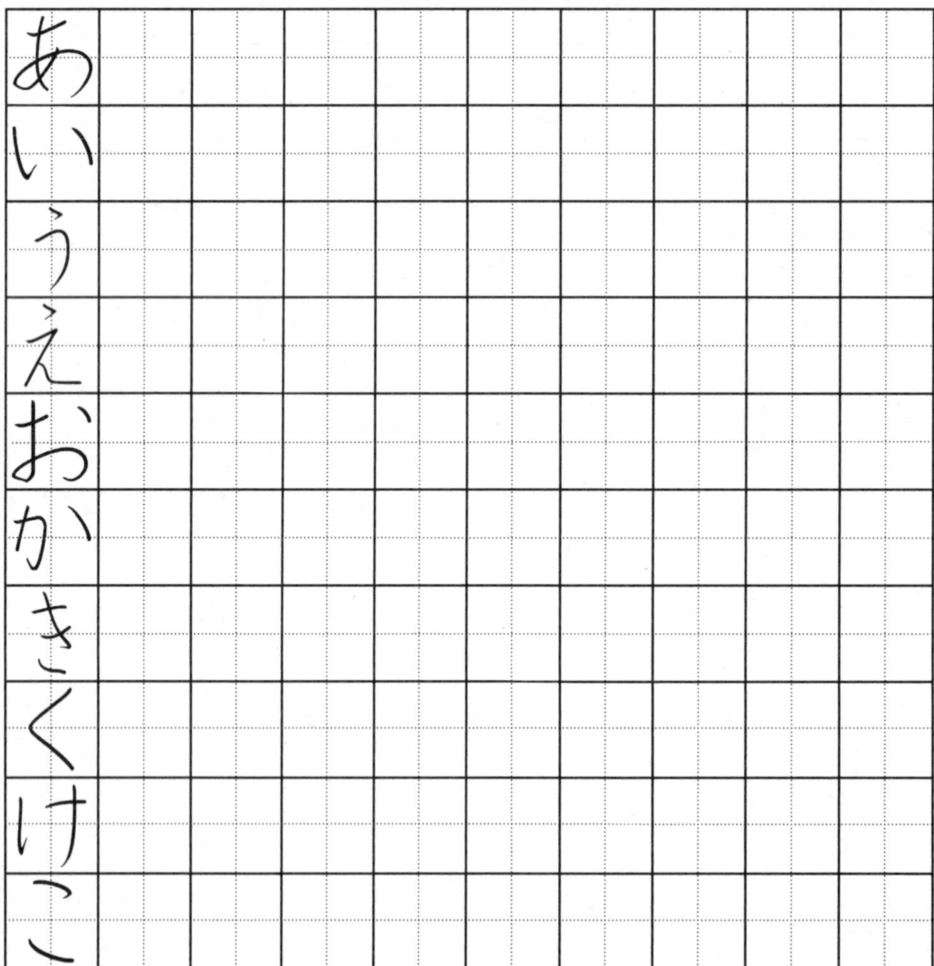


 

Name ______________________ Class ______________ Date ________________

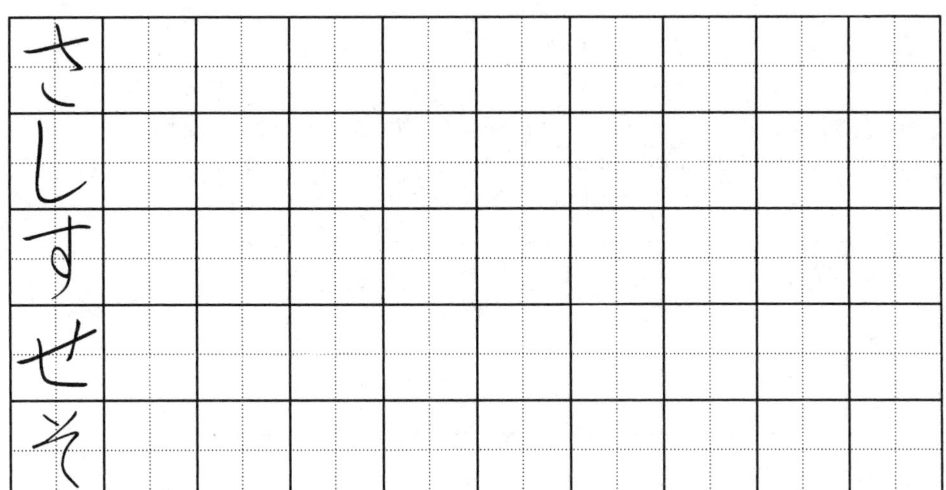


C. Write the following words in **hiragana**.

**1.** kasa (*umbrella*) ______________________

**2.** kiku (*chrysanthemum*) ______________________

**3.** isu (*chair*) ______________________

**4.** oka (*hill*) ______________________

**5.** kisoku (*rule*) ______________________

**6.** ashi (*leg*) ______________________

**7.** uso (*lie*, n.) ______________________

**8.** koe (*voice*) ______________________

**9.** ike (*pond*) ______________________

**10.** sekai (*world*) ______________________

## II. Hiragana た〜ほ

A. Write each **hiragana**, following the correct stroke order. The arrows indicate the direction of each stroke. Pay attention to the balance of each character and how each stroke ends, *Stop* (S), *Release* (R), or *Hook* (H). R/S indicates individual variations.

Name ______________________ Class ______________ Date ________________

B. Practice writing each **hiragana**, following the correct stroke order. Work from top to bottom to avoid writing the same character repeatedly.

| た | | | | | | | | | |
|---|---|---|---|---|---|---|---|---|---|
| ち | | | | | | | | | |
| つ | | | | | | | | | |
| て | | | | | | | | | |
| と | | | | | | | | | |
| な | | | | | | | | | |
| に | | | | | | | | | |
| ぬ | | | | | | | | | |
| ね | | | | | | | | | |
| の | | | | | | | | | |
| は | | | | | | | | | |
| ひ | | | | | | | | | |
| ふ | | | | | | | | | |
| へ | | | | | | | | | |
| ほ | | | | | | | | | |

C. Write the following words in **hiragana**.

**1.** tsuchi (*soil*) ______________________

**2.** nasu (*eggplant*) ______________________

**3.** hachi (*bee*) ______________________

**4.** nuka (*rice bran*) ______________________

**5.** nokosu (*to save*) ______________________

**6.** hito (*person*) ______________________

**7.** tane (*seed*) ______________________

**8.** hifu (*skin*) ______________________

**9.** fune (*ship*) ______________________

**10.** hoshikusa (*hay*) ______________________

Name ______________________________ Class ____________________ Date ____________________

# III. Hiragana ま〜ん

A. Write each **hiragana**, following the correct stroke order. The arrows indicate the direction of each stroke. Pay attention to the balance of each character and how each stroke ends, *Stop* (S), *Release* (R), or *Hook* (H). H/S indicates individual variations.

| | | | |
|---|---|---|---|
| ま | S | S | S |
| み | S | R | |
| む | S | R | H/S |
| め | S | R | |
| も | R | H/S | S |
| や | R | H/S | S |
| ゆ | R | R | |
| よ | S | S | |
| ら | H/S | R | |
| り | H/S | R | |
| る | S | | |
| れ | S | R | |
| ろ | R | | |
| わ | S | R | |
| を | S | S | S |
| ん | R | | |

B. Practice writing each **hiragana,** following the correct stroke order. Work from top to bottom to avoid writing the same character repeatedly.

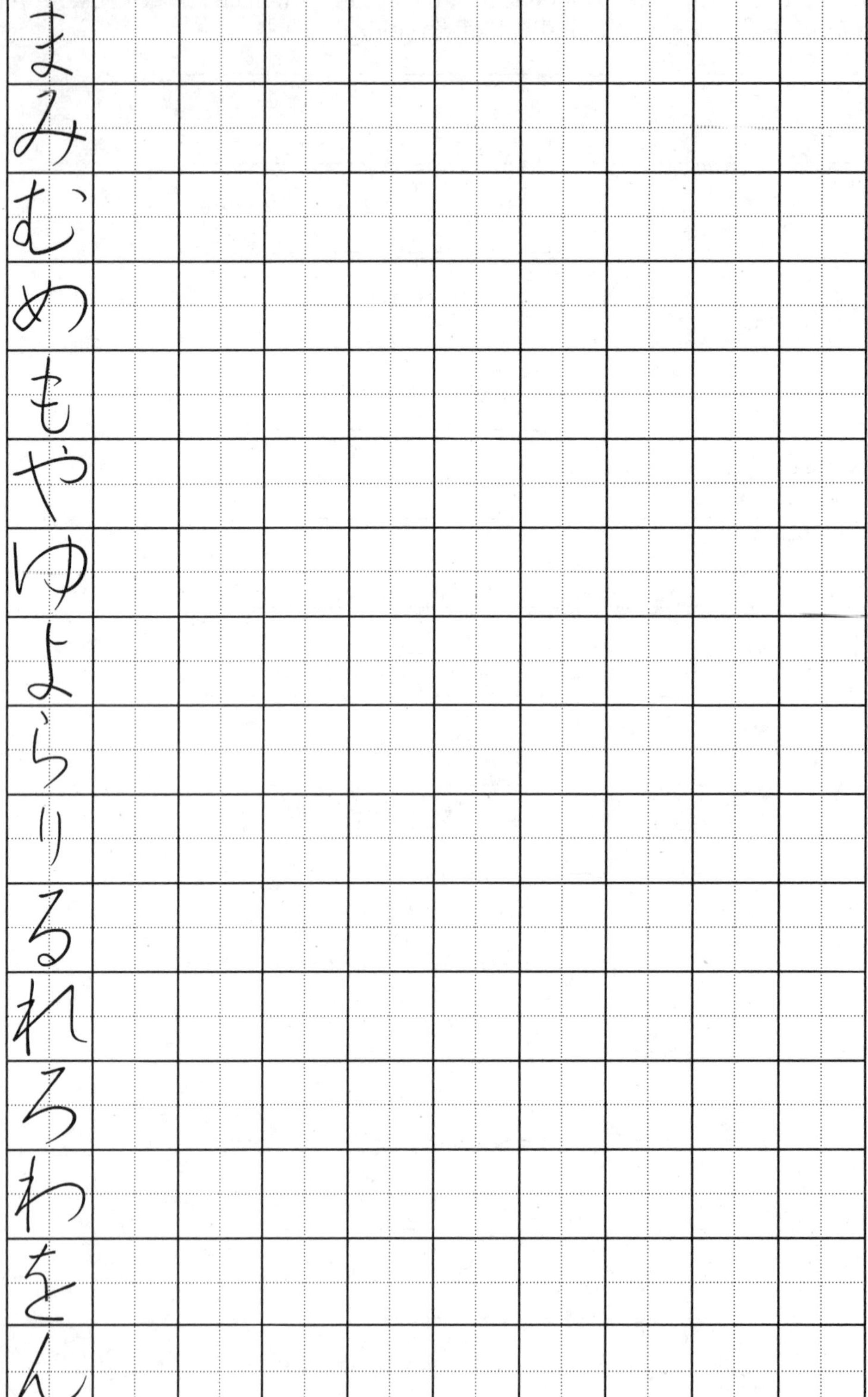

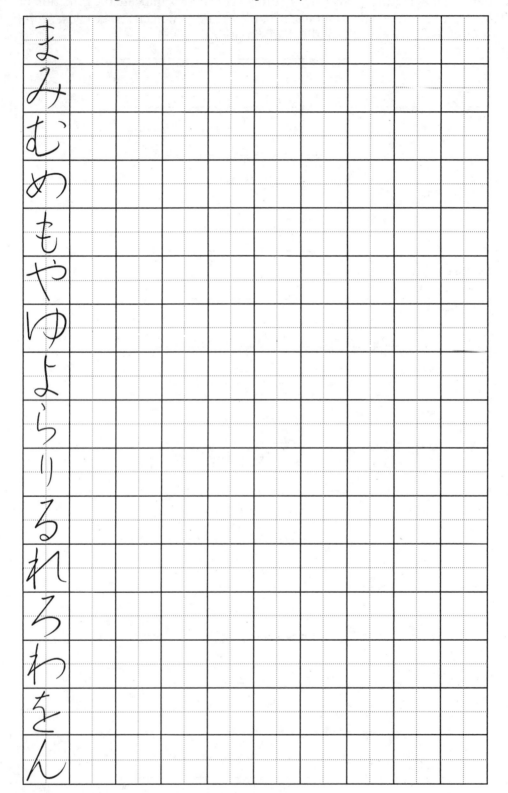

 

Name ______________________ Class ______________ Date ______________

# ラボの　れんしゅう　**Lab Activities**

## I. Introduction and Hiragana あ～そ

A. Listen to and repeat each of the following words or phrases. After you hear each one a second time, write it down. Stop the audio as necessary.

| | | |
|---|---|---|
| 1. ______ | 7. ______ | 13. ______ |
| 2. ______ | 8. ______ | 14. ______ |
| 3. ______ | 9. ______ | 15. ______ |
| 4. ______ | 10. ______ | 16. ______ |
| 5. ______ | 11. ______ | 17. ______ |
| 6. ______ | 12. ______ | 18. ______ |

B. Listen to and repeat each of the following words, paying attention to the whispered sounds.

| | |
|---|---|
| **1.** きし *shore* | **5.** すそ *hem* |
| **2.** きく *chrysanthemum* | **6.** すき *like* |
| **3.** くき *stalk* | **7.** しき *four seasons* |
| **4.** くさ *grass* | **8.** しか *deer* |

C. You are attending an orientation session for international students at a university in Japan. Some of the students approach you and introduce themselves. Following the example, greet each person and give your name.

■ You hear: はじめまして。かとう　です。どうぞ　よろしく。
(hajimemashite katoo desu doozo yoroshiku)

You say: はじめまして。ぶらうん　です。どうぞ　よろしく。
(hajimemashite buraun desu doozo yoroshiku)

## II. Hiragana た～ほ

A. Listen to and repeat each of the following words or phrases. After you hear each one a second time, write it down. Stop the audio as necessary.

1. ______ 7. ______ 13. ______
2. ______ 8. ______ 14. ______
3. ______ 9. ______ 15. ______
4. ______ 10. ______ 16. ______
5. ______ 11. ______ 17. ______
6. ______ 12. ______ 18. ______

B. Listen to and repeat each of the following words, paying attention to the whispered sound.

**1.** つち *soil* **5.** ちか *underground*

**2.** つき *moon* **6.** ちち *my father*

**3.** かつ *to win* **7.** さちこ *Sachiko (female name)*

**4.** まつ *to wait for*

C. You run into some of your classmates and instructors on campus at various times of the day. They greet you. Give each person the appropriate response. You will then hear the correct response.

■ You hear: 9:00 a.m., おはよう ございます。 (ohayoo gozaimasu)

You say: おはよう ございます。 (ohayoo gozaimasu)

You hear: おはよう ございます。 (ohayoo gozaimasu)

D. You run into some of your classmates and instructors during the day. After hearing the cue telling you the time of day, greet each person. You will then hear the correct greeting.

■ You hear: 3:00 p.m.

You say: こんにちは。 (konnichiwa)

You hear: こんにちは。 (konnichiwa)

 

Name ______________________ Class ________________ Date __________________

# III. Hiragana ま〜ん

A. Listen to and repeat each of the following words or phrases. After you hear each one a second time, write it down. Stop the audio as necessary.

| | | |
|---|---|---|
| 1. ____________ | 7. ____________ | 13. ____________ |
| 2. ____________ | 8. ____________ | 14. ____________ |
| 3. ____________ | 9. ____________ | 15. ____________ |
| 4. ____________ | 10. ____________ | 16. ____________ |
| 5. ____________ | 11. ____________ | 17. ____________ |
| 6. ____________ | 12. ____________ | 18. ____________ |

B. Listen to and repeat each of the following words, paying attention to the [n] sounds. You will then hear the word again.

| | |
|---|---|
| **1.** あに *elder brother* | **4.** こんな *this kind (of)* |
| **2.** あんい *easygoing* | **5.** たね *seed* |
| **3.** こな *powder* | **6.** たんねん *detailed* |

C. Your last class is over and you are going home. You see some of your classmates and instructors in the hallway and expect to see them again soon. Listen to each cue identifying a classmate or an instructor and greet that person appropriately. You will then hear the correct greeting.

■ You hear: やまださん (y a m a d a s a n)

You say: じゃあ、また。 (j a a m a t a)

You hear: じゃあ、また。 (j a a m a t a)

## IV. Hiragana が〜ぽ: Voiced consonants

A. Listen to and repeat each of the following words or phrases. After you hear each one a second time, write it down. Stop the audio as necessary.

1. ____________ 7. ____________ 13. ____________

2. ____________ 8. ____________ 14. ____________

3. ____________ 9. ____________ 15. ____________

4. ____________ 10. ____________ 16. ____________

5. ____________ 11. ____________ 17. ____________

6. ____________ 12. ____________ 18. ____________

B. Listen to each of the following pairs of words and identify which word in the pair has a voiced sound. Circle first or second. Listen to the model:

■ You hear: から、がら
You see: first second
You circle: *second*, because the second word you heard had a voiced sound.

1. first second
2. first second
3. first second
4. first second
5. first second
6. first second

C. Listen to and repeat each of the following phrases, paying attention to the length of each sound. You will then hear the phrase again.

D. What would you say in each of the following situations? Listen to each cue identifying a situation and respond appropriately. You will then hear the correct response.

■ You hear: You lost a book that you borrowed from a friend.

You say: すみません。

You hear: すみません。

 

Name ______________ Class ______________ Date ______________

## V. Hiragana ああ～わあ : Long vowels

A. Listen to and repeat each of the following words or phrases. After you hear each one a second time, write it down. Stop the audio as necessary.

1. ______________ 7. ______________ 13. ______________

2. ______________ 8. ______________ 14. ______________

3. ______________ 9. ______________ 15. ______________

4. ______________ 10. ______________ 16. ______________

5. ______________ 11. ______________ 17. ______________

6. ______________ 12. ______________

B. Listen to and repeat each of the following words or phrases. After you hear each one a second time, write it down. Stop the audio as necessary.

1. ______________________________

2. ______________________________

3. ______________________________

4. ______________________________

5. ______________________________

C. Listen to the following pairs of words and repeat them, paying attention to the contrast in pronunciation for each pair.

| | | | | |
|---|---|---|---|---|
| **1.** | え | *picture* | ええ | *yes* |
| **2.** | い | *stomach* | いい | *good* |
| **3.** | いえ | *house* | いいえ | *no* |
| **4.** | すし | *sushi* | すうし | *numeral* |
| **5.** | さと | *countryside* | さとう | *sugar* |
| **6.** | きれ | *cloth* | きれい | *pretty, clean* |
| **7.** | くつ | *shoes* | くつう | *pain* |
| **8.** | かぜ | *wind* | かぜい | *taxation* |
| **9.** | おばさん | *aunt* | おばあさん | *grandmother* |
| **10.** | おじさん | *uncle* | おじいさん | *grandfather* |
| **11.** | ここ | *here* | こうこう | *high school* |
| **12.** | しゅじん | *my husband* | しゅうじん | *prisoner* |

D. Listen to Professor Yamamoto's requests. Write the letter of the illustration that matches each request.

**A.**

**B.**

**C.**

**D.**

**E.**

■ You hear: きいて　ください

You write: A because the request means *please listen.*

**1.** ________ **5.** ________

**2.** ________ **6.** ________

**3.** ________ **7.** ________

**4.** ________ **8.** ________

 

Name ______________________ Class ______________ Date ______________

# VI. Hiragana Small っ : Double consonants

A. Listen to the following pairs of words or phrases and identify which word or phrase in each pair contains a double consonant. Circle *first* or *second*.

■ You hear: いって、いて

You see: first second

You circle: *first*, because the first word you heard had a double consonant.

1. first second
2. first second
3. first second
4. first second
5. first second
6. first second
7. first second

B. Listen to the following pairs of words and identify each word that contains a double consonant. Circle *first*, *second*, *both*, or *neither*.

■ You hear: さか、さか

You see: first second both neither

You circle: *neither*, because neither word you heard had a double consonant.

1. first second both neither
2. first second both neither
3. first second both neither
4. first second both neither
5. first second both neither
6. first second both neither

C. Listen to the following words or phrases first in English, then in Japanese. Repeat each of the Japanese words or phrases. After you hear it a second time, write it down. Stop the audio as necessary.

■ You hear: school, がっこう

You repeat: がっこう

You hear: がっこう

You write: がっこう

1. ______________________________

2. ______________________________

3. ______________________________

4. ______________________________

5. ______________________________

6. ______________________________

7. ______________________________

8. ______________________________

D. A Japanese friend is speaking to you but you don't understand everything he says. Ask him to speak louder or slower or to repeat what he said, depending on what you hear. You will then hear the correct request. Repeat each request.

■ You hear: こんにちは。

You say: もうすこし　ゆっくり　おねがいします。

You hear: もうすこし　ゆっくり　おねがいします。

You repeat: もうすこし　ゆっくり　おねがいします。

 

Name ________________________ Class ________________ Date ________________

# VII. Hiragana きゃ〜ぴょ : Glides

A. Listen to the following pairs of words and identify which word in each pair has a glide. Circle first or second.

■ You hear: りょう、りよう

You see: first second

You circle: *first*, because the first word you heard had a glide.

1. first second
2. first second
3. first second
4. first second
5. first second
6. first second

B. Listen to the following pairs of words and identify which words have a glide. Circle first, second, both, or neither.

■ You hear: さか、しゃか

You see: first second both neither

You circle: *second*, because the second word you heard had a glide.

1. first second both neither
2. first second both neither
3. first second both neither
4. first second both neither
5. first second both neither
6. first second both neither

C. Listen to the following words first in English, then in Japanese. Repeat each of the Japanese words, then write it down after you hear it a second time. Stop the audio as necessary.

■ You hear: homework, しゅくだい

You repeat: しゅくだい

You hear: しゅくだい

You write: しゅくだい

1. ____________________

2. ____________________

3. ____________________

4. ____________________

5. ____________________

6. ____________________

7. ____________________

 

Name ______________________ Class ______________ Date ______________

## Chapter 2
だいにか

# Greetings and Introductions

# あいさつと　じこしょうかい

## Workbook Activities

### たんごの　れんしゅう　Vocabulary Practice

Look at the clocks below and write the time next to each one.

■ Example

いちじです。

1. ごじです。

2. はちじ

3. じゅうじ

4. よじはんです。

5. じゅうじはんです

Name ____________________ Class ______________ Date ______________

## I. Identifying someone or something, using ～は　～です

Imagine that you have a pen pal in Japan and that the following people live in your dormitory. Write a short description of each student to your pen pal. You may use **hiragana** for the words written in **katakana**.

| なまえ<br>**Name** | ～じん<br>**Nationality** | ～ねんせい<br>**Year in school** | せんこう<br>**Major** |
|---|---|---|---|
| ブラウン<br>ぶらうん | アメリカじん<br>あめりか | いちねんせい | こうがく |
| キム<br>きむ | かんこくじん | だいがくいんせい | ビジネス<br>びじねす |
| チョー<br>ちょ | ちゅうごくじん | にねんせい | えいご |
| モネ<br>もね | カナダじん<br>かなだ | よねんせい | アジアけんきゅう<br>あじあ |
| スミス<br>すみす | オーストラリアじん<br>お　すとらりあ | さんねんせい | ぶんがく |

■ Example　ブラウンさんは　アメリカじんです。いちねんせいです。
(ぶらうん / あめりか)
せんこうは　こうがくです。

1. キムさんは ______________。______________。
(きむ)

せんこうは ______________。

2. チョーさんは ______________。______________。
(ちょ)

せんこうは ______________。

3. モネさんは ______________。______________。
(もね)

______________________________。

4. スミスさんは ______________。______________。
(すみす)

______________________________。

Name ________________ Class ________________ Date ________________

## III. Indicating relationships between nouns with の

Imagine that you are writing to your Japanese pen pal about your friends from Japan. Look at the chart below and write something about each student, following the example.

| なまえ<br>Name | だいがく<br>University | ～ねんせい<br>Year in school | せんこう<br>Major |
|---|---|---|---|
| やまだ | おおさかだいがく | さんねんせい | えいご |
| おおき | とうきょうだいがく | だいがくいんせい | こうがく |
| さとう | じょうとうだいがく | よねんせい | かんこくご |
| たなか | きょうとだいがく | にねんせい | ぶんがく |
| いとう | にほんだいがく | いちねんせい | れきし |
| はやし | なごやだいがく | だいがくいんせい | スペインご<br>すぺいん |
| すずき | わせだだいがく | さんねんせい | ちゅうごくご |

■ Example

やまださんは　おおさかだいがくの　さんねんせいです。

やまださんの　せんこうは　えいごです。

1. おおきさんは ________________________________。

________________________________。

2. さとうさんは ________________________________。

________________________________。

3. たなかさんは ________________________________。

________________________________。

4. いとうさんは ________________________________。

________________________________。

5. はやしさんは ________________________________。

________________________________。

6. すずきさんは ________________________________。

________________________________。

Name ______________________ Class ______________ Date ______________

## IV. Asking for personal information using question words

A. Complete the following dialogue, using the appropriate question words.

■ Example A: やまださんは　どこから　きましたか。

B: とうきょうから　きました。

A: あのう、すみません。(1) ______________________。

B: やまだです。

A: はじめまして、わたしは　たなかです。どうぞ　よろしく。

B: こちらこそ、どうぞ　よろしく。たなかさんは　がくせいですか。

A: ええ、そうです。やまださんは。

B: わたしも　がくせいです。じょうとうだいがくの　さんねんせいです。

(2) ______________________。

A: わたしの　だいがくは　きょうとだいがくです。せんこうは　こうがくです。

(3) ______________________。

B: アジア(あじあ)けんきゅうです。(4) ______________________。

A: よねんせいです。

B: そうですか。これからも　どうぞ よろしく。

A: こちらこそ。

B. Look at the map to answer questions about the time in different cities.

■ Example

A: とうきょうは　いま　なんじですか。

B: ごぜん　じゅういちじです。

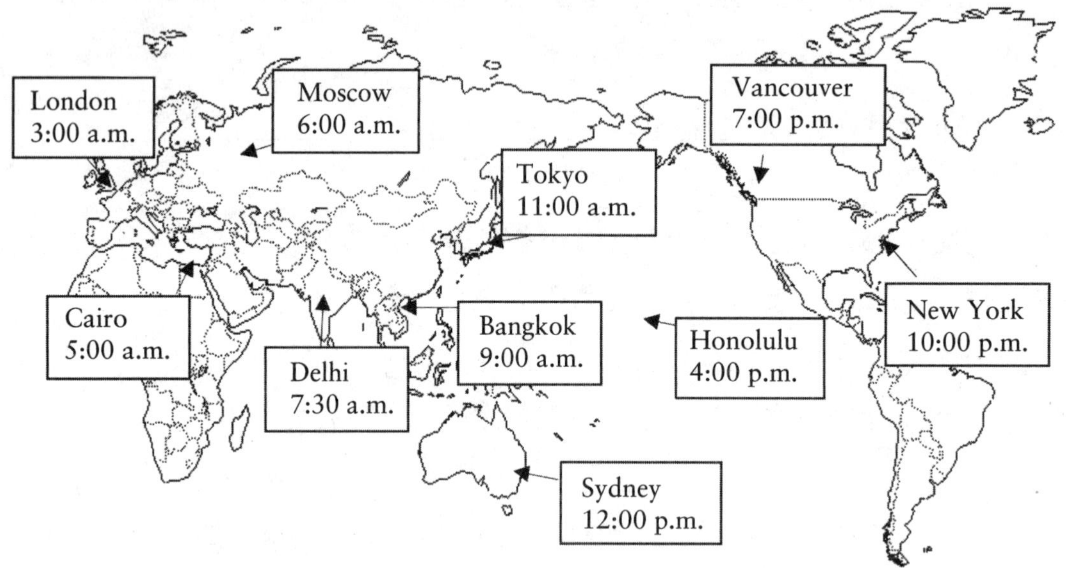


1. バンコク (*Bangkok*)
ばんこく

A: バンコクは　いま　なんじですか。
ばんこく

B: ______________________________________________。

2. シドニー (*Sydney*)
しどに

A: シドニーは　いま　なんじですか。
しどに

B: ______________________________________________。

3. モスクワ (*Moscow*)
もすくわ

A: モスクワは　いま　なんじですか。
もすくわ

B: ______________________________________________。

4. ロンドン (*London*)
ろんどん

A: ロンドンは　いま　なんじですか。
ろんどん

B: ______________________________________________。

5. デリー (*Delhi*)
でり

A: デリーは　いま　なんじですか。
でり

B: ______________________________________________。

 

## V. Using も to list and describe similarities

The following is a list of new students at the International Student Center. Look at the chart and use も to complete the sentences. You may use **hiragana** for the words written in **katakana**.

| なまえ<br>**Name** | くに<br>**Country** | ～ねんせい<br>**Year in school** | せんこう<br>**Major** |
|---|---|---|---|
| キム<br>きむ | かんこく | いちねんせい | フランスご<br>ふらんす |
| イー<br>い | かんこく | だいがくいんせい | ぶんがく |
| リー<br>り | ちゅうごく | よねんせい | こうがく |
| チョー<br>ちょ | ちゅうごく | にねんせい | かんこくご |
| ブラウン<br>ぶらうん | オーストラリア<br>お すとらりあ | さんねんせい | れきし |
| スミス<br>すみす | オーストラリア<br>お すとらりあ | にねんせい | かんこくご |
| ロペス<br>ろぺす | メキシコ<br>めきしこ | よねんせい | フランスご<br>ふらんす |
| ガルシア<br>がるしあ | メキシコ<br>めきしこ | だいがくいんせい | こうがく |
| ワット<br>わっと | イギリス<br>いぎりす | いちねんせい | れきし |
| モリス<br>もりす | イギリス<br>いぎりす | さんねんせい | ぶんがく |

■ Example　キムさんは　かんこくから　きました。

イー(い)さんも　かんこくから　きました。

**1.** リー(り)さんは ______________________________ からきました。

チョー(ちょ)さん ______________________________________。

**2.** チョー(ちょ)さんは ____________________________ ねんせいです。

スミス(すみす)さん ______________________________________。

**3.** ガルシア(がるしあ)さんは __________________________ せいです。

_____________________________________________。

4. モリスさんは ______________________ せいです。
   もりす

______________________________________。

5. ブラウンさんの　せんこうは ______________________。
   ぶらうん

   ワットさん ______________________________。
   わっと

6. リーさんの　せんこうは ______________________。
   り

______________________________________。

 

Name ______________________ Class ______________ Date ______________

# そうごうれんしゅう Integration

Mr. Tanaka and Mr. Kimura have just met each other at a party at the Westside University International Student Center. Complete their conversation, using the information from the following chart.

| なまえ<br>**Name** | だいがく<br>**University** | ～ねんせい<br>**Year in school** | せんこう<br>**Major** | ～からきました<br>**Hometown** |
|---|---|---|---|---|
| たなか | じょうとうだいがく | さんねんせい | えいご | とうきょう |
| きむら | にほんだいがく | いちねんせい | えいご | こうべ |

たなか：あのう、すみません。にほんじんですか。

きむら：ええ、そうですけど。

たなか：はじめまして。ぼく、たなかです。どうぞ　よろしく。

きむら：________________。きむらです。__________________________。

たなか：きむらさんは　がくせいですか。

きむら：______、______________。にほんだいがくの　いちねんせいです。

たなか：そうですか。ぼくは　__________________ さんねんせいです。
せんこうは　えいごです。

きむら：そうですか。____________________ えいごです。

__________________________。

たなか：とうきょうから　きました。きむらさんは　どこから　きましたか。

きむら：________________________________________。

たなか：そうですか。あ、あのう、すみませんが、

________________________________________。

きむら：いちじはんですよ。

たなか：そうですか。______________________________。

きむら：いいえ。

Name ______________________ Class ______________ Date ______________

# ラボの　れんしゅう Lab Activities

## Part 1: Vocabulary

Please turn to the vocabulary list on pages a-32–a-35 of your textbook and repeat each word or phrase you hear.

## Part 2: Speaking and Listening Comprehension Activities

### I. Identifying someone or something, using ～は～です

A. Look at the chart containing information about four people. Then listen to the following statements about them. Stop the audio as necessary. If a statement is true, circle はい. If it is false, circle いいえ.

■ You hear: さとうさんは　だいがくせいです。

You see and choose: (はい)　いいえ

| Name | さとう | モネ (もね) | キム (きむ) | ブラウン (ぶらうん) |
|---|---|---|---|---|
| Status | だいがくせい | だいがくせい | せんせい | がくせい |
| Nationality | アメリカじん (あめりか) | カナダじん (かなだ) | かんこくじん | オーストラリアじん (お すとらりあ) |
| Year in school | さんねんせい | いちねんせい | N/A | だいがくいんせい |

1. はい　いいえ
2. はい　いいえ
3. はい　いいえ
4. はい　いいえ
5. はい　いいえ
6. はい　いいえ
7. はい　いいえ
8. はい　いいえ

B. Look at the chart in Activity A again. You will hear a cue consisting of a name and nationality, or a name and academic status or year in school. If the cue matches the information in the chart, respond orally, using ～は　～です. If the cue doesn't match the information in the chart, respond using ～は　～じゃ　ありません or ～じゃないです. You will then hear the correct response. Write the correct response when you hear it.

■ You hear: さとう / せんせい

You say: さとうさんは　せんせいじゃありません。

or さとうさんは　せんせいじゃないです。

You hear: さとうさんは　せんせいじゃありません。

or さとうさんは　せんせいじゃないです。

You write: さとうさんは　せんせいじゃありません。

or さとうさんは　せんせいじゃないです。

1. ______________________________

2. ______________________________

3. ______________________________

4. ______________________________

5. ______________________________

 

Name ______________________ Class ________________ Date __________________

## II. Asking はい／いいえ questions, using ～は　～ですか

Using the chart below, answer each question orally. You will then hear the correct answer. Stop the audio and write the answer.

■ You hear: チョーさんは　せんせいですか。
ち ょ

You say: いいえ、そうじゃありません。

or いいえ、そうじゃないです。

You hear: いいえ、そうじゃありません。

or いいえ、そうじゃないです。

You write: いいえ、そうじゃありません。

or いいえ、そうじゃないです。

| **Name** | チョー<br>ち ょ | ロペス<br>ろ ぺ す | スミス<br>す み す | ブラウン<br>ぶ ら う ん |
|---|---|---|---|---|
| **Status** | だいがくせい | だいがくせい | せんせい | がくせい |
| **Nationality** | ちゅうごくじん | メキシコじん<br>め き し こ | オーストラリアじん<br>お す と ら り あ | アメリカじん<br>あ め り か |
| **Year in school** | いちねんせい | よねんせい | N/A | だいがくいんせい |

1. ______________________________________________

2. ______________________________________________

3. ______________________________________________

4. ______________________________________________

5. ______________________________________________

Name ______________________________ Class __________________ Date ____________________

## III. Indicating relationships between nouns with の

Imagine that there are five scholars from Japan at your school this year. They are from different universities and teach different subjects. Listen to the information about each scholar and write the appropriate choice from the list in order to complete the table. Stop the audio as necessary.

■ You hear: たなかせんせいの　だいがくは　とうきょうだいがくです。

| | University | Subject |
|---|---|---|
| たなか | (とうきょう) だいがく | (　　　　　　) |
| やまだ | (　　　　　　) だいがく | (　　　　　　) |
| きむら | (　　　　　　) だいがく | (　　　　　　) |
| いとう | (　　　　　　) だいがく | (　　　　　　) |
| おおき | (　　　　　　) だいがく | (　　　　　　) |

**Universities:** とうきょう　わせだ　きょうと　にほん　おおさか

**Subjects:** こうがく　れきし　ぶんがく　かんこくご　えいご

Name ______________________ Class ______________ Date ______________

## IV. Asking for personal information, using question words

A: Listen to the following personal questions and write your answers in Japanese. Stop the audio as necessary.

■ You hear: せんこうは　なんですか。
You write: にほんごです。

1. ______________________________

2. ______________________________

3. ______________________________

4. ______________________________

5. ______________________________

B: You are at the airport and ask someone about the times in various cities. Listen to the dialogues and write the times as shown in the model.

■ You hear: A: すみません、ホンコン(ほんこん)は　いま　なんじですか。
B: ごご　にじですよ。

You write: ホンコン(ほんこん) (*Hong Kong*) 2:00 PM

1. ロンドン(ろんどん) (*London*) ______________

2. ニューヨーク(にゅよく) (*New York*) ______________

3. バンコク(ばんこく) (*Bangkok*) ______________

4. とうきょう ______________

Name ______________________ Class ______________ Date ______________

## V. Using も to list and describe similarities

Listen to some statements about the people in the following chart. After hearing each one, find another person in the chart who shares the same characteristic and make a sentence using the particle も. You will then hear the correct answer. Stop the audio and write it down.

| なまえ **Name** | スミスさん (すみす) | ブラウンさん (ぶらうん) | リーさん (り) | モネさん (もね) |
|---|---|---|---|---|
| ～じん **Nationality** | アメリカじん (あめりか) | アメリカじん (あめりか) | カナダじん (かなだ) | カナダじん (かなだ) |
| ～ねんせい **Year in school** | だいがくせい | だいがくいんせい | だいがくせい | だいがくいんせい |
| せんこう **Major** | アジアけんきゅう (あじあ) | こうがく | こうがく | アジアけんきゅう (あじあ) |
| だいがく **University** | UCLA | おおさかだいがく | UCLA | おおさかだいがく |
| しゅっしん **Hometown** | シカゴ (Chicago) (しかご) | シカゴ (しかご) | トロント (Toronto) (とろんと) | トロント (とろんと) |

■ You hear: スミスさんは　だいがくせいです。

You say: リーさんも　だいがくせいです。

You hear: リーさんも　だいがくせいです。

You write: リーさんも　だいがくせいです。

1. ______________________________

2. ______________________________

3. ______________________________

4. ______________________________

5. ______________________________

Name ____________________ Class ______________ Date ______________

## Part 3: Dict-a-Conversation

The Dict-a-Conversation combines listening and writing practice in a conversational format. This activity is done with the audio, either as homework or lab work. You will hear one side of a conversation about a topic covered in the chapter. After writing down what you hear, you will create your side of the conversation. (See the steps below.) In the Dict-a-Conversation your last name is Smith (スミス(すみす)), unless you are told otherwise. For this chapter, use only **hiragana** when you write your part of the lines.

**Step 1** Listen carefully to what your conversation partner says. You may listen to the recorded audio as many times as you wish.

**Step 2** Write the lines of your partner (きむら, やまだ, etc.) as you hear them.

**Step 3** Next, write your own responses, questions, or statements on the appropriate lines.

**Step 4** When you have finished, read through the completed script to check your work.

A. You are meeting the father of your host family, Mr. Kimura, at Narita Airport for the first time.

きむら：________________________________

スミス(すみす)：________________________________

きむら：________________________________

________________________________

B. At a party you meet a young Japanese woman whose name is Yamada. Converse with her.

やまだ：________________________________

スミス(すみす)：________________________________

やまだ：________________________________

スミス(すみす)：________________________________

やまだ：________________________________

スミス(すみす)：________________________________

Name ______________________ Class ______________ Date ________________

# Chapter 2.5

# カタカナ

# Katakana

## Workbook Activities

### Katakana ア〜ソ

A. Write each **katakana**, following the correct stroke order. The arrows indicate the direction of each stroke. Pay attention to the balance of each character and how each stroke ends, *Stop* (S), *Release* (R), or *Hook* (H). H/S or R/S indicates individual variations.

| | | | |
|---|---|---|---|
| ア | H/S | R | |
| イ | R | S | |
| ウ | S | S | R |
| エ | S | S | S |
| オ | S | H | R |
| カ | H | R | |
| キ | S | S | S |
| ク | R/S | R | |
| ケ | R | S | R |
| コ | S | S | |

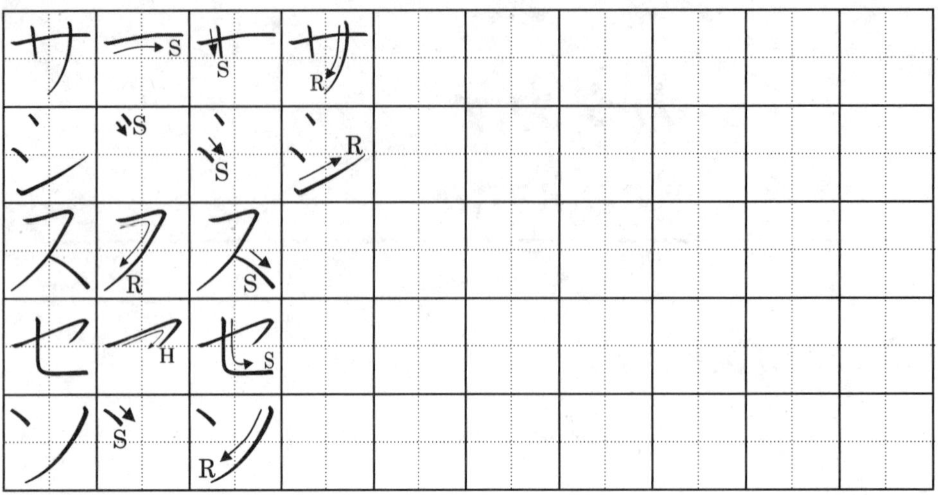


B. Practice writing each **katakana**, following the correct stroke order. Write different characters in order, rather than writing the same character repeatedly.

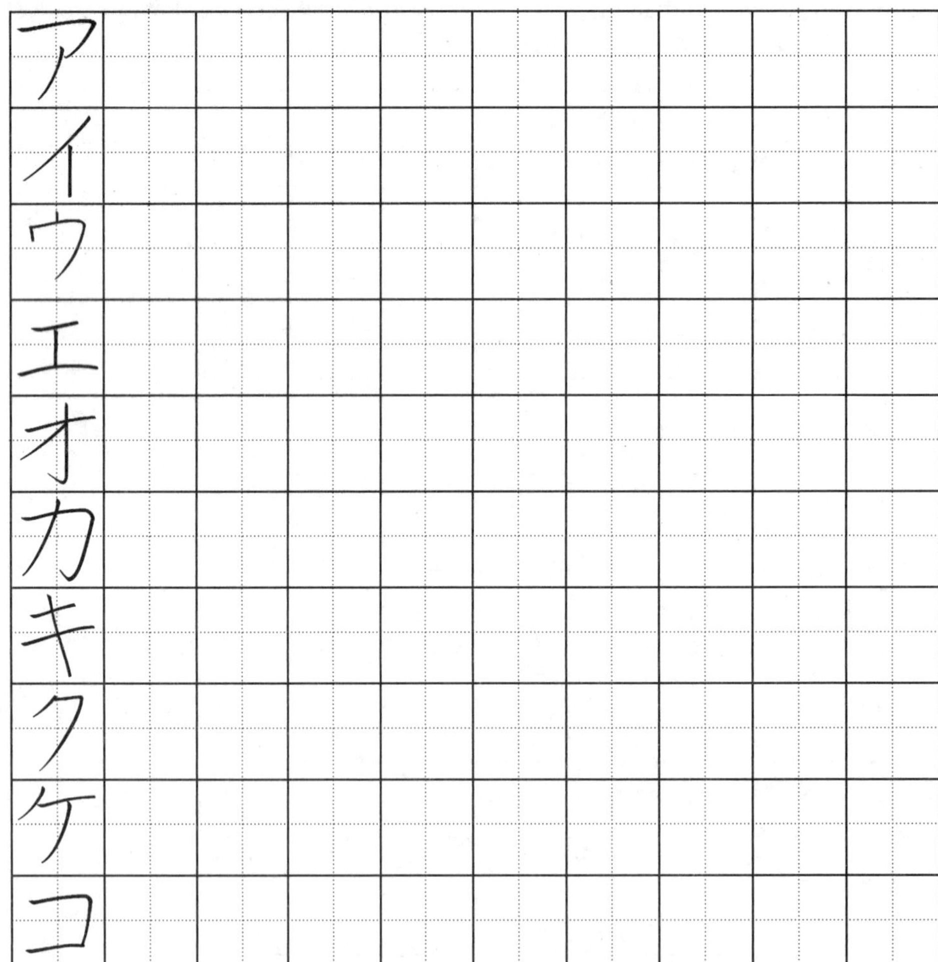


 

Name ____________ Class ____________ Date ____________

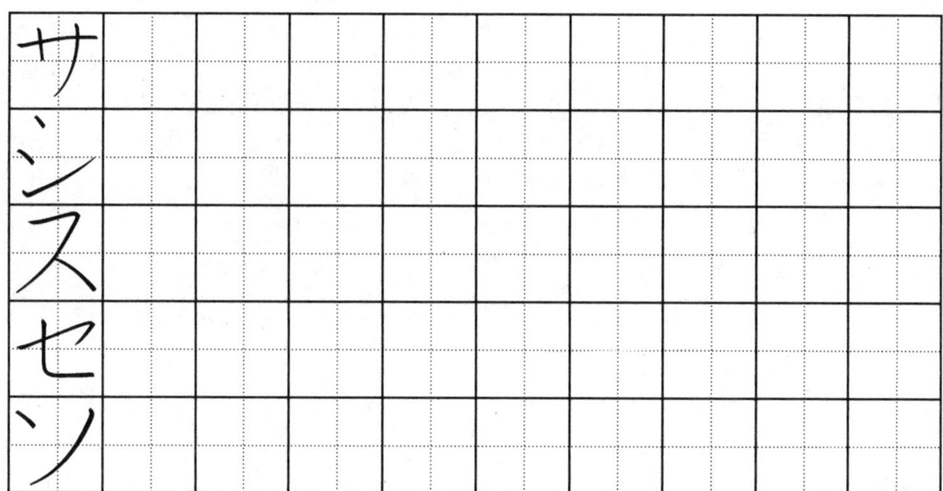


C. Practice writing each **katakana** word five times, then guess its meaning in English.

■ Example スイス スイス スイス スイス スイス スイス
Switzerland

1. ケーキ ____________

2. スキー ____________

3. ケース ____________

4. シーソー ____________

5. オアシス ____________

D. Transcribe the following **hiragana** words into **katakana** and guess their English meanings.

■ Example えーす エース ace

1. きす ____________ ____________

2. さーかす ____________ ____________

3. ここあ ____________ ____________

4. あいす ____________ ____________

5. こーす ____________ ____________

## Katakana　タ～ホ

A. Write each **katakana**, following the correct stroke order. The arrows indicate the direction of each stroke. Pay attention to the balance of each character and how each stroke ends, *Stop* (S), *Release* (R), or *Hook* (H). R/S indicates individual variations.

Name ______________________ Class ______________ Date ______________

B. Practice writing each **katakana,** following the correct stroke order. Write different characters in order, rather than writing the same character repeatedly.

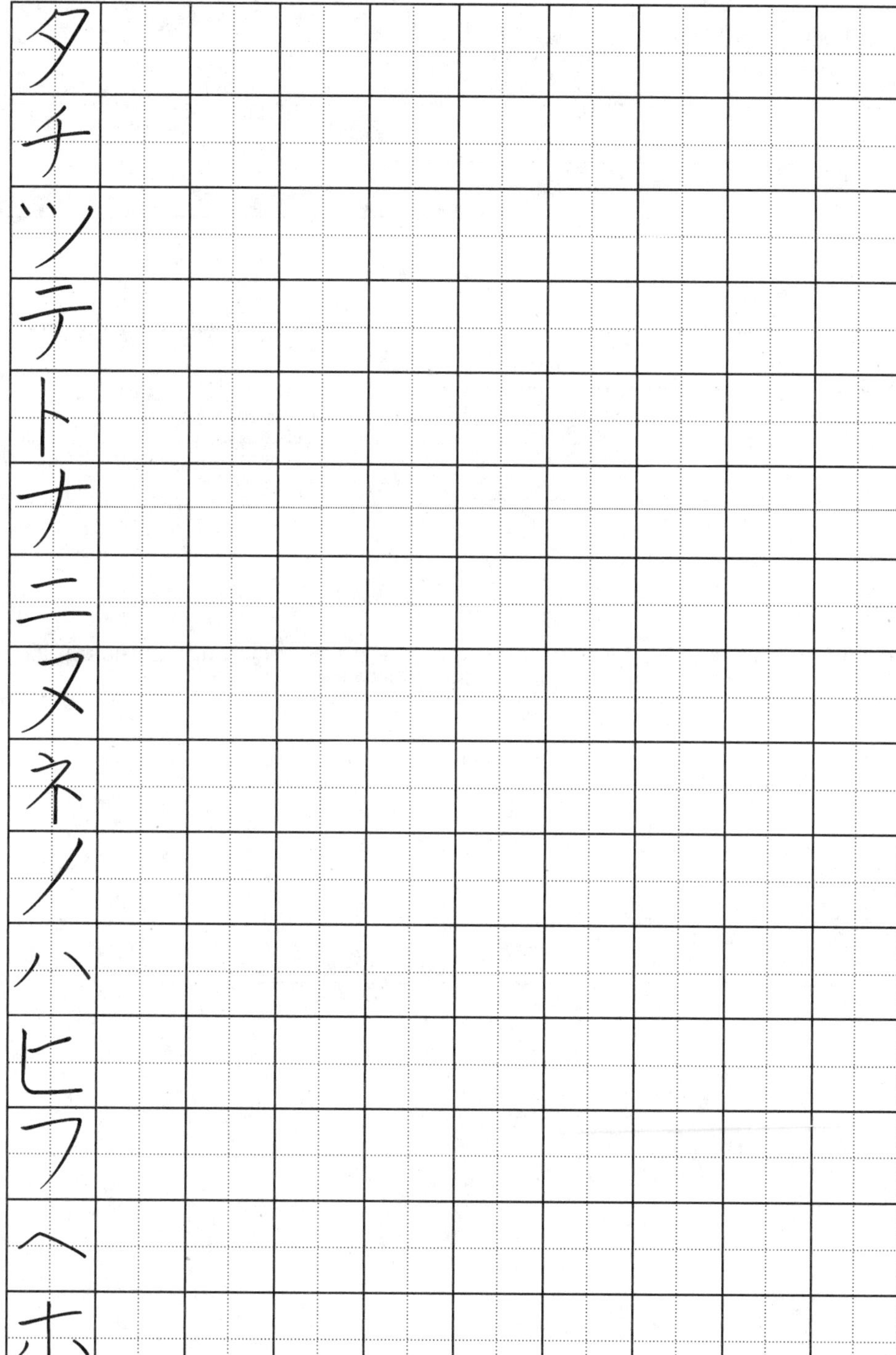

C. Practice writing each **katakana** word five times, then guess its meaning in English.

■ Example カット　　カット　カット　カット　カット　カット
cut

1. テスト ____________________

2. セーター ____________________

3. カヌー ____________________

4. ノート ____________________

5. ヒーター ____________________

D. Transcribe the following **hiragana** words into **katakana** and guess their English meanings.

■ Example ほっと　ホット　hot

1. ねっと ________ ________
2. たっち ________ ________
3. てきさす ________ ________
4. おはいお ________ ________
5. えちけっと ________ ________

 

Name ____________________ Class ______________ Date ______________

# カタカナ　マ〜ン

A. Write each **katakana**, following the correct stroke order. The arrows indicate the direction of each stroke. Pay attention to the balance of each character and how each stroke ends, *Stop* (S), *Release* (R), or *Hook* (H). R/S indicates individual variations.

| | | | | | | | | | |
|---|---|---|---|---|---|---|---|---|---|
| マ | R/S | S | | | | | | | |
| ミ | S | S | S | | | | | | |
| ム | S | S | | | | | | | |
| メ | R | S | | | | | | | |
| モ | S | S | S | | | | | | |
| ヤ | H | S | | | | | | | |
| ユ | S | S | | | | | | | |
| ヨ | S | S | S | | | | | | |
| ラ | S | R | | | | | | | |
| リ | S | R | | | | | | | |
| ル | R | H | | | | | | | |
| レ | H | | | | | | | | |
| ロ | S | S | S | | | | | | |
| ワ | S | R | | | | | | | |
| ン | S | R | | | | | | | |

B. Practice writing each **katakana**, following the correct stroke order. Write different characters in order, rather than writing the same character repeatedly.

| | | | | | | | | | |
|---|---|---|---|---|---|---|---|---|---|
| マ | | | | | | | | | |
| ミ | | | | | | | | | |
| ム | | | | | | | | | |
| メ | | | | | | | | | |
| モ | | | | | | | | | |
| ヤ | | | | | | | | | |
| ユ | | | | | | | | | |
| ヨ | | | | | | | | | |
| ラ | | | | | | | | | |
| リ | | | | | | | | | |
| ル | | | | | | | | | |
| レ | | | | | | | | | |
| ロ | | | | | | | | | |
| ワ | | | | | | | | | |
| ン | | | | | | | | | |

 

Name ______________ Class ______________ Date ______________

C. Practice writing each **katakana** word five times, then guess its meaning in English.

1. アメリカ ______________________________

______________

2. フランス ______________________________

______________

3. メキシコ ______________________________

______________

4. ステレオ ______________________________

______________

5. レストラン ______________________________

______________

D. Transcribe the following **hiragana** words into **katakana** and guess their English meanings.

1. いたりあ ______________ ______________
2. らーめん ______________ ______________
3. あふりか ______________ ______________
4. くりすます ______________ ______________
5. おーすとらりあ ______________ ______________

# カタカナの　ふくしゅう (Summary of Katakana)

A. The following words appear in Chapter 2 of your textbook. Write them out in **katakana** (and **hiragana if necessary**).

**1.** Asian studies ____________________ **4.** business ____________________

**2.** Canada ____________________ **5.** Spain ____________________

**3.** England ____________________

B. Read these **katakana** words and write their meanings in English.

■ Example　コーラ　　<u>cola</u>

**1.** ニューヨーク ______________ **7.** ギャップ ______________

**2.** シドニー ______________ **8.** ピザハット ______________

**3.** エンジニア ______________ **9.** バーガーキング ______________

**4.** コンピュータ ______________ **10.** ウォルマート ______________

**5.** トイザラス ______________ **11.** フェデックス ______________

**6.** マクドナルド ______________ **12.** クリスピークリーム ______________

C. Transcribe the following **hiragana** words into **katakana** and guess their English meanings.

**1.** かたろぐ ______________ ______________

**2.** だいびんぐ ______________ ______________

**3.** ぴんぽん ______________ ______________

**4.** すとろべりー ______________ ______________

**5.** とらんぺっと ______________ ______________

**6.** けんぶりっじ ______________ ______________

**7.** あっぷるぱい ______________ ______________

**8.** ばいおりん ______________ ______________

**9.** ちきんすーぷ ______________ ______________

**10.** ちょこれーと ______________ ______________

**11.** ちゃんす ______________ ______________

**12.** じょぎんぐ ______________ ______________

 

13. おれんじじゅーす ______________ ______________

14. しゃーべっと ______________ ______________

15. まさちゅーせっつ ______________ ______________

16. しゃんぷー ______________ ______________

17. にゅーじーらんど ______________ ______________

18. こみゅにけーしょん ______________ ______________

D. Transcribe the following romanized words into **katakana** and guess their English meanings. Refer to page a-80 of your textbook for the **katakana** combinations.

1. finrando ______________ ______________
2. kariforunia ______________ ______________
3. noruwee ______________ ______________
4. dizunii rando ______________ ______________
5. supagetti ______________ ______________
6. sheekusupia ______________ ______________
7. foomaru wea ______________ ______________
8. weetoresu ______________ ______________

E. Write your full name, state, country, and hometown in both English and **katakana**.

Name (first and last) ______________________________

State/Country ______________________________

Hometown ______________________________

Name ______________ Class ______________ Date ______________

# ラボの　れんしゅう Lab Activities

## Katakana ア～ソ

Listen to each of the following words and repeat them. You will then hear the word again. Write each word. Stop the audio as necessary.

1. ______________
2. ______________
3. ______________
4. ______________
5. ______________
6. ______________
7. ______________
8. ______________
9. ______________

## Katakana タ～ホ

Listen to each of the following words and repeat them. You will then hear the word again. Write each word. Stop the audio as necessary.

1. ______________
2. ______________
3. ______________
4. ______________
5. ______________
6. ______________
7. ______________
8. ______________
9. ______________
10. ______________
11. ______________

Name ______________________ Class ______________ Date ______________

## Katakana マ〜ン

Listen to each of the following words and repeat them. You will then hear the word again. Write each word. Stop the audio as necessary.

1. ______________________ 7. ______________________

2. ______________________ 8. ______________________

3. ______________________ 9. ______________________

4. ______________________ 10. ______________________

5. ______________________ 11. ______________________

6. ______________________ 12. ______________________

## カタカナの　ふくしゅう (Summary of Katakana)

Listen to each of the following words and repeat them. You will then hear the word again. Write each word. Stop the audio as necessary.

1. ______________________ 14. ______________________

2. ______________________ 15. ______________________

3. ______________________ 16. ______________________

4. ______________________ 17. ______________________

5. ______________________ 18. ______________________

6. ______________________ 19. ______________________

7. ______________________ 20. ______________________

8. ______________________ 21. ______________________

9. ______________________ 22. ______________________

10. ______________________ 23. ______________________

11. ______________________ 24. ______________________

12. ______________________ 25. ______________________

13. ______________________

Name ______________________ Class ______________ Date ______________

Chapter 3
だいさんか

# Daily Routines

# まいにちの　せいかつ

## Workbook Activities

### たんごの　れんしゅう Vocabulary Practice

A. Suppose today is **October 10.** Answer the following questions.

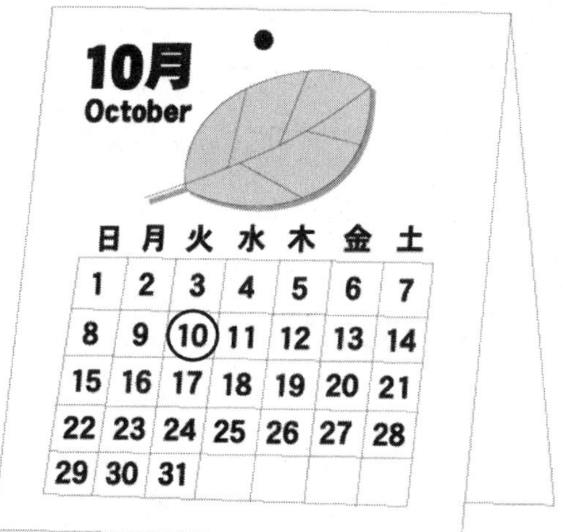


**1.** きょうは　なんようびですか。

______________________________________________

**2.** あさっては　なんようびですか。

______________________________________________

**3.** きのうは　なんようびでしたか。( でした =was )

______________________________________________

B. Rewrite the following numbers in hiragana.

1. 17 ______________________

2. 51 ______________________

3 99 ______________________

4. 64 ______________________

5. 23 ______________________

C. Write the following time expressions in hiragana.

1. 9:50 ______________________________________

2. 11:15 ______________________________________

3. 12:03 ______________________________________

4. 10:38 p.m. ______________________________________

5. 4:29 a.m. ______________________________________

6. 7:36 p.m. ______________________________________

Name ______________________ Class ________________ Date ________________

## I. Talking about routines, future actions, or events using the polite present form of verbs and the particles に, へ, を, or で

A. Complete the table below by writing the polite present forms of the verbs in the left-hand column.

| English verb | Polite affirmative form | Polite negative form |
|---|---|---|
| to go | いきます | いきません |
| to eat | | |
| to come | | |
| to return | | |
| to go to bed | | |
| to read | | |
| to see | | |
| to enter; to take (a bath) | | |
| to wake up | | |
| to do | | |

B. Complete the sentences by filling in the parentheses and the blanks with the correct particle (を, に, へ) and the most appropriate verb from the list below.

いきます　よみます　のみます　はいります　たべます　します　みます

■ Example　あさごはん（を）＿＿たべます＿＿。

1. ほん（　　）＿＿＿＿＿＿＿＿＿＿。
2. おふろ（　　）＿＿＿＿＿＿＿＿＿＿。
3. ジュース (*juice*)（　　）＿＿＿＿＿＿＿＿＿＿。
4. テレビ（　　）＿＿＿＿＿＿＿＿＿＿。
5. しゅくだい（　　）＿＿＿＿＿＿＿＿＿＿。
6. がっこう（　　）＿＿＿＿＿＿＿＿＿＿。

C. Complete the sentences by filling in each parenthesis with the correct particle.

■ Example コーヒー（を）のみます。

1. どこ（　　）いきますか。

2. シャワー（　　）あびます。

3. うち（　　）ねます。

4. きょう　なに（　　）しますか。

5. アパート (*apartment*)（　　）かえります。

6. としょかん（　　）べんきょうします。

7. レストラン (*restaurant*)（　　）なに（　　）たべますか。

8. どこ（　　）えいが（　　）みますか。

Name ______________________ Class ______________ Date ________________

## II. Presenting objects or events using ～が　あります

After reading each exchange, fill in the parentheses and the blanks with the appropriate particle or the verb あります.

1. A: しゅうまつ　コンサート(こんさと) (*concert*)　(　　)　ありますよ。

   B: どこ (　　)　ありますか。

   A: こうえん (*park*)　(　　)　あります。

2. A: たなかさん、きょう　じゅぎょう　(　　)ありますか。

   B: ええ、ビジネス(びじねす)　(　　)じゅぎょう (　　)　______________。

   A: そうですか。どこ　(　　)　______________ か。

   B: アレンホール(あれんほる) (*Allen Hall*)　(　　)　______________。

## III. Telling time using the particle に

Answer the following questions.

1. まいあさ　なんじに　おきますか。

   ______________________________________________。

2. まいにち　なんじごろ　ばんごはんを　たべますか。

   ______________________________________________。

3. いつ　だいがくに　いきますか。

   ______________________________________________。

4. なんようびに　にほんごの　じゅぎょうが　ありますか。

   ______________________________________________。

5. にほんごの　じゅぎょうは　なんじなんぷんに　ありますか。

   ______________________________________________。

Name ______________________ Class ______________ Date ______________

## IV. Using adverbs to express frequency of actions

A. Complete the sentences by filling in the parentheses with the correct particles, and put the most appropriate verbs from the list into the blanks. Change the verb into the negative form if necessary.

| します | はいります | いきます | たべます | よみます | かえります |
|---|---|---|---|---|---|
| おきます | みます | ねます | | | |

■ Example テレビ（てれび）（を）あまり みません 。

1. ほん（　　）よく ______________。
2. ときどき レストラン（れすとらん）(*restaurant*)（　　）ひるごはん（　　）______________。
3. たいてい　あさ　ろくじ（　　）______________。
4. えいが（　　）あまり ______________。
5. たいてい　ごご　ごじ（　　）うち（　　）______________。
6. すずきさんは　ぜんぜん　おふろ（　　）______________。
7. さとうさんは　いつも　ごご　じゅういちじ（　　）______________。
8. スミス（すみす）さんは　あまり　べんきょう ______________。
9. やまださんは　ぜんぜん　じゅぎょう（　　）______________。

B. Answer the following questions about your daily routine using frequency expressions.

■ Example　としょかんに　よく　いきますか。

はい、ときどき　いきます。 or いいえ、あまり　いきません。 etc.

1. いつも　あさ　シャワー(しゃわ)を　あびますか。

______________________________。

2. よく　にほんごの　ほんを　よみますか。

______________________________。

3. よく　としょかんで　べんきょうしますか。

______________________________。

4. よく　おふろに　はいりますか。

______________________________。

5. よく　テレビ(てれび)を　みますか。

______________________________。

6. いつも　あさごはんを　たべますか。なんじごろ　たべますか。

______________________________。

Name ______________________________ Class ___________________ Date ____________________

## V. Expressing past actions and events using the polite past form of verbs

A. Complete the following table by writing the polite past forms of the verbs in the left-hand column.

| Polite present affirmative form | Polite past affirmative form | Polite past negative form |
|---|---|---|
| おきます | おきました | おきませんでした |
| のみます | | |
| あびます | | |
| かえります | | |
| おきます | | |
| いきます | | |
| はいります | | |
| きます | | |
| あります | | |
| します | | |

B. The pictures below show what Mr. Tanaka did yesterday. Write sentences describing his activities.

■ Example

7:30　　たなかさんは　しちじはんに　おきました。

1. 

8:15

2. 

9:30

3. 

(at the library) 11:30

4. 

4:40

5. 

(at home) 7:00

6. 

12:30

1. ______________________________

2. ______________________________

3. ______________________________

4. ______________________________

5. ______________________________

6. ______________________________

 

Name ______________________ Class ______________ Date ______________

# そうごうれんしゅう Integration

Read the passage below describing a typical week of a teacher's life. Then answer the questions that follow. Look only for the specific words or phrases you need to answer the questions. Don't worry about trying to understand all of the information!

山本先生(やまもとせんせい)は日本語(にほんご)の先生(せんせい)です。先生(せんせい)は毎朝七時(まいあさしちじ)ごろ起(お)きます。たいてい朝(あさ)ごはんを食(た)べます。でも、きのうは時間(じかん)がありませんでしたから、食(た)べませんでした。いつも八時(はちじ)ごろ大学(だいがく)に行(い)きます。先生(せんせい)は九時半(くじはん)に一年生(いちねんせい)の日本語(にほんご)の授業(じゅぎょう)があります。そして、十一時(じゅういちじ)に三年生(さんねんせい)の日本語(にほんご)の授業(じゅぎょう)があります。よく学食(がくしょく) (*school cafeteria*) で昼(ひる)ごはんを食(た)べます。そして、毎日五時(まいにちごじ)にうちに帰(かえ)ります。夜(よる)はたいていうちで晩(ばん)ごはんを食(た)べます。テレビ(てれび)はぜんぜん見(み)ません。週末(しゅうまつ)にときどきデパート(でぱと)に行(い)って、映画(えいが)を見(み)ます。きのうも日本(にほん)の映画(えいが)を見(み)ました。

**1.** やまもとせんせいは　なんじに　おきますか。

しちじごろ(に) おきます。

**2.** せんせいは　きのう　あさごはんを　たべましたか。

いいえ、たべませんでした。

**3.** いつ　だいがくに　いきますか。

はちじごろに いきます。

**4.** なんじに　さんねんせいの　にほんごの　じゅぎょうが　ありますか。

じゅういちじに ~~じゅぎょうが~~ あります。

**5.** どこで　ばんごはんを　たべますか。

(たいてい)うちで たべます。

**6.** せんせいは　よく　テレビ(てれび)を　みますか。

いいえ、ぜんぜんみません。

**7.** せんせいは　きのう　えいがを　みましたか。

はい、みました。

Name ______________________ Class ______________ Date ______________

# ラボの　れんしゅう Lab Activities

## Part 1: Vocabulary

Please turn to the vocabulary list on pages a-84–a-87 of your textbook and repeat each word or phrase you hear.

## Part 2: Vocabulary Practice

A. Listen and write the numbers you hear in Arabic numerals.

**1.** ~~98~~ 78  **3.** ~~94~~ 14  **5.** 39

**2.** 76  **4.** 28  **6.** 91

B. Listen and write the time expressions you hear in Arabic numerals.

■ You hear: ごぜんいちじ

You write: 1:00 a.m.

**1.** 4:35  **5.** 3:30 p.m  **8.** 7:51 am

**2.** 9:13 am  **6.** 8:16 p.m  **9.** 3:44 pm  3:44

**3.** 12:20  **7.** 11:30 am  **10.** 10:07 pm

**4.** 6:58

Name ______________________ Class ______________ Date ________________

## Part 3: Speaking and Listening Comprehension Activities

### I. Talking about routines, future actions, and events using the polite present form of verbs and the particles に, へ, を, or で

A. Create a sentence using the words you hear. Supply the correct particles.

■ You hear: テレビ(てれび)　みます

You say: テレビ(てれび)を　みます。

You hear: テレビ(てれび)を　みます。

B. Form a question using the words you hear. Supply the correct particles. Then answer the question using the cue you hear.

■ You hear: なに　よみます

You say: なにを　よみますか。

You hear: なにを　よみますか。

You repeat: なにを　よみますか。

You hear: ほん

You say and write: ほんを　よみます。

1. ______________________________________________

2. ______________________________________________

3. ______________________________________________

4. ______________________________________________

5. ______________________________________________

6. ______________________________________________

Name ______________________ Class ______________ Date ________________

## II. Presenting objects or events using ～が　あります

Listen to each of the following questions and answer each question first orally, then in writing.

1. ________________________________________________

2. ________________________________________________

3. ________________________________________________

4. ________________________________________________

## III. Telling time using the particle に

A. Look at Mr.Yamada's schedule below, and answer the questions.

■ You hear: やまださんは　なんじに　おきますか。
You say and write: しちじに　おきます。

| | |
|---|---|
| 7:00 a.m. | おきます |
| 7:30 a.m. | シャワー(しゃわ)を　あびます。 |
| 8:10 a.m. | だいがくに　いきます。 |
| 8:35 a.m. | にほんごの　じゅぎょうが　あります。 |
| 12:30 p.m. | ひるごはんを　たべます。 |
| 1:25 p.m. | ぶんがくの　じゅぎょうが　あります。 |
| 4:00 p.m. | うちに　かえります。 |

1. ________________________________________________

2. ________________________________________________

3. ________________________________________________

4. ________________________________________________

5. ________________________________________________

6. ________________________________________________

B. Look at Mr. Suzuki's schedule. Listen to a statement and circle はい if it is true and いいえ if it is false.

■ You hear : すずきさんは　はちじに　おきます。

You see: はい　いいえ

You circle: はい, because Mr. Suzuki wakes up at eight o'clock.

8:00 a.m. 　8:30 a.m. 　9:15 a.m. 　10:00 a.m. history class

12:00 p.m. 　1:30 p.m. 　4:00 p.m. 　6:30 p.m.

9:00 p.m. 　12:30 a.m.

1. はい　いいえ　　4. はい　いいえ
2. はい　いいえ　　5. はい　いいえ
3. はい　いいえ　　6. はい　いいえ

C. Look at Mr. Suzuki's schedule again and answer the following questions using はい、～ます or いいえ、～ません.

■ You hear: すずきさんは　はちじに　おきますか。

You say and write: はい、おきます。

1. ______________________　4. ______________________

2. ______________________　5. ______________________

3. ______________________　6. ______________________

Name ______________________ Class ______________ Date ________________

## IV. Using adverbs to express frequency of actions

A. Listen, then form a sentence with the frequency adverbs you hear.

■ You hear: あさごはんを　たべます。/ よく

You say: よく　あさごはんを　たべます。

You hear: よく　あさごはんを　たべます。

B. Listen to the following exchanges between Mr. Johnson and Ms. Kimura. Complete each statement based on the context of the conversation.

■ You hear: ジョンソン(じょんそん)：きむらさんは　どこで　べんきょうしますか。

きむら：そうですね。としょかんで　よく　べんきょうしますね。ジョンソンさんは。

ジョンソン(じょんそん)：ぼくは　としょかんでは　ぜんぜん　べんきょうしません。でも、よく　がくせいかいかん (*student union*) で　します。

You write: きむらさんは　よく　としょかんで　べんきょうします。

ジョンソン(じょんそん)さんは　ぜんぜん　としょかんで　べんきょうしません。

**1.** きむらさんは __________ きっさてんに __________________。

ジョンソン(じょんそん)さんも __________ きっさてんに　いきません。

**2.** きむらさんは __________ おふろに　はいります。

ジョンソン(じょんそん)さんは __________ おふろに ________________。

**3.** きむらさんは __________ コーヒー(こひ)を ________________。

ジョンソン(じょんそん)さんは __________ コーヒー(こひ)を　のみます。

**4.** きむらさんは __________ あさごはんを ________________。

ジョンソン(じょんそん)さんは __________ あさごはんを ________________。

**5.** きむらさんは __________ えいがを ________________。

ジョンソン(じょんそん)さんは __________ えいがを ________________。

Name ______________________ Class ______________ Date ______________

## V. Expressing past actions and events using the polite past form of verbs

A. Listen to each of the following questions and cues. Answer each question orally, using the cue. You will then hear the correct answer.

■ You hear: きのう　ほんを　よみましたか。/ いいえ

You say: いいえ、よみませんでした。

You hear: いいえ、よみませんでした。

B. Listen to the following exchanges. After each one, fill in the blank to complete the statement about the exchange.

■ You hear: おとこのひと (*man*)：　きのう　なんじに　ねましたか。

おんなのひと (*woman*)：じゅういちじはんに　ねました。

You write: おんなのひとは　きのう　じゅういちじはんに　ねました。

**1.** おんなのひとは　きのう ________________ で ____________________。

**2.** おんなのひとは　きのう ____________ ごろ ____________ を ________________。

**3.** おんなのひとは　きのう ________ の ____________ を ________________。

Name ______________________ Class ______________ Date ______________

## Part 4: Dict-a-Conversation

Imagine that you, Smith, are on your college campus and you run into your friend Mr. Suzuki around lunch time. Listen to what Mr. Suzuki says to you. Then write it down and add your replies.

すずき：________________________________________

スミス（すみす）：________________________________________

すずき：________________________________________

スミス（すみす）：________________________________________

すずき：________________________________________

スミス（すみす）：________________________________________

すずき：________________________________________

スミス（すみす）：________________________________________

すずき：________________________________________

Name ____________________ Class ______________ Date ______________

# Chapter 4
# だいよんか

# Japanese Cities

# にほんの　まち

## Workbook Activities

### たんごの　れんしゅう　Vocabulary Practice

A. Answer the following questions in Japanese.

**1.** よく　カフェに　いきますか。

______________________________

**2.** カフェで　なにを　しますか。

______________________________

**3.** せんしゅう、デパートに　いきましたか。

______________________________

**4.** 大学(だいがく)の　ほんやに　よく　いきますか。

______________________________

**5.** こんしゅう、にほんごの　テストが　ありますか。どこで　ありますか。

______________________________

B. Complete the following sentences by using the most appropriate adjective from the list ＋ です.

■ Example　わたしの　うちは　大(おお)きいです。

1. わたしの　大学(だいがく)は　____________________。

2. ニューヨークの　まちは　____________________。

3. わたしの　かばんは　____________________。

4. イチロー (*Ichiro Suzuki*) は　____________________。

5. わたしの　にほんごの　きょうかしょは　____________________。

| | | | |
|---|---|---|---|
| あたらしい | ふるい | ちいさい | 大(おお)きい |
| きれい | ゆうめい | りっぱ | あかい |
| あおい | くろい | しろい | ちゃいろい |

Name ______________________ Class ______________ Date ________________

## I. Referring to things using これ，それ，あれ，どれ

A. Mr. Smith and Ms. Kimura are talking about various things. Look at the drawing and complete their conversation, using これ, それ, あれ or other appropriate words.

スミス： あのう、すみません。__________は　にほんごで　なんと　いいますか。

きむら： けしゴムと　いいます。

スミス： そうですか。じゃあ、__________________は　なんと　いいますか。

きむら： これですか。　これは　えんぴつと　いいます。

スミス： そうですか。じゃあ、__________________は　なんですか。

きむら： __________________は　じしょです。

スミス： __________________は　なんと　いいますか。

きむら： かばんと　いいます。

スミス： そうですか。__________________は　*notebook* と　いいますか。

きむら： いいえ、________________は　ノートって　いいます。__________は　スミスさんの　ノートですか。

スミス： ええ、そうです。_____________は___________の　かばんですか。

きむら： やまださんの　かばんですよ。

スミス： じゃあ、____________________も　やまださんの　じしょですか。

きむら： いいえ、わたしの　じしょです。

B. Look at the map below. Mr. Yamada (A) is showing Mr. Kim (B) around the town. They are now standing right in front of the police station. Complete their conversation using これ, それ, あれ, どれ.

キム：　やまださん、________は　なんですか。

やまだ：きっさてんです。

キム：　じゃあ、____________は　大学(だいがく)ですか。

やまだ：いいえ、___________は　びょういんの　たてものですよ。

キム：　そうですか。　りっぱですね。______________は　なんですか。

やまだ：_____________は　ぎんこうですよ。

キム：　大(おお)きいですね。じゃあ、ほんやは___________ですか。

やまだ：ほんやですか？　ほんやは___________です。

 

Name ______________________ Class ________________ Date ________________

## II. Asking for and giving locations using ～は　～に　あります／います and ここ，そこ，あそこ

A. Look at the drawing of a street. You and your friend Mr. Tanaka are standing in front of the police box. Mr. Tanaka asks you about different places in the neighborhood. Answer his questions using ここ, そこ, あそこ.

■ Example A: としょかんは　どこに　ありますか。
B: そこ／あそこに　あります。

1. A: こうえんは　どこに　ありますか。
B: ______________________________

2. A: ゆうびんきょくは　どこに　ありますか。
B: ______________________________

3. A: ほんやは　どこに　ありますか。
B: ______________________________

4. A: きっさてんは　どこに　ありますか。
B: ______________________________

B. Answer the following questions using ～に　あります.

■ Example　じょうとう大学(だいがく)は　どこに　ありますか。

　　　　　<u>とうきょうに　あります。</u>

1. ～さん (*you*) の　うちは　どこに　ありますか。

______________________________

2. おとうさん (*your father*) は　どこに　いますか。

______________________________

3. ディズニーランドは　どこに　ありますか。

______________________________

4. いま、にほんごの　先生(せんせい)は　どこに　いますか。

______________________________

5. よく　レストランに　いきますか。なにを　たべますか。
レストランは　どこに　ありますか。

______________________________

______________________________

　

Name ______________________________ Class ___________________ Date _____________________

C. Fill in the parentheses with the appropriate particles. If nothing is appropriate, write an x instead.

**1.** スミス： たなかさん（　　）りょう（　　）、どこ（　　）ありますか。

たなか： あそこ（　　）あります。

**2.** A: こんばん、えいが（　　）ありますよ。

B: どこ（　　）ありますか。

A: スミスホール（　　）あります。

B: そうですか。なんじ（　　）ありますか。

A: えーっと、はちじ（　　）ありますよ。

**3.** A: ブラウンさん（　　）いま、どこ（　　）いますか。

B: としょかん（　　）いますよ。

A: ああ、そうですか。

**4.** ブラウン： すずきさん、いま、じゅぎょう（　　）いきますか。

すずき： ええ、アレンホール（　　）にほんご（　　）じゅぎょう（　　）あります。

ブラウン： そうですか。アレンホール（　　）どれ（　　）ですか。

すずき： あれ（　　）ですよ。

Name ______________________ Class ______________ Date ________________

## III. Describing people and things using adjectives + noun, and polite present forms of adjectives

A. Write your answer to each of the following questions, choosing from the adjectives in the box. Follow the model.

| 大(おお)きい ちいさい あたらしい ふるい あかい あおい くろい しろい |
|---|
| たかい いい きれい(な) りっぱ(な) ゆうめい(な) |

■ Example ～さん (*you*) の 大学(だいがく)は どんな 大学(だいがく)ですか。

ちいさい 大学(だいがく)です。

1. ～さんの 大学(だいがく)は どんな 大学(だいがく)ですか。

_______________________________________________

2. 大学(だいがく)の ほんやは どんな たてものですか。

_______________________________________________

3. ～さんの かばんは どんな かばんですか。

_______________________________________________

4. ～さんの ボールペンは どんな ボールペンですか。

_______________________________________________

B. Complete the following chart by writing the appropriate adjective forms.

| Dictionary form | Polite affirmative form | Polite negative form | Adjective + Noun |
|---|---|---|---|
| 大(おお)きい | 大(おお)きいです | 大(おお)きくありません | 大(おお)きい　うち |
| ちいさい | | | うち |
| ゆうめい | | | うち |
| いい | | | うち |
| あたらしい | | | うち |
| りっぱ | | | うち |
| きれい | | | うち |
| ちゃいろい | | | うち |
| ふるい | | | うち |

C. Answer the following questions, using the appropriate forms of the adjectives and adverbs.

■ Example　～さん (*you*) の　大学(だいがく)は　大(おお)きいですか。

<u>ええ、とても　大(おお)きいです。</u>

**1.** ～さんの　大学(だいがく)は　ふるいですか。

________________________________________

**2.** 大学(だいがく)の　としょかんは　りっぱですか。

________________________________________

**3.** 大学(だいがく)の　りょうは　いいですか。

________________________________________

**4.** ～さんの　まちの　スーパーは　きれいですか。

________________________________________

**5.** ～さんの　じしょは　ふるいですか。

________________________________________

Name ______________________ Class ________________ Date ________________

D. Complete the following conversations using the appropriate words.

■ Example たなか：さとうさん、さとうさんの　大学(だいがく)は　大(おお)きいですか。

さとう：ええ、とても　<u>大(おお)きいですよ</u>。

1. ブラウン：かとうさんの　りょうは　りっぱですか。

かとう：　いいえ、あまり________________。

2. A: スミスさんの　うちは　きれいですね。

B: ええ、とても________________ね。

3. うえだ：たなかさんの　とけい (*watch*) は　とても________________ね。

たなか：ええ、わたしの　おばあさん (*grandmother*) の　とけいですよ。アンティーク (*antique*) です。

4. A: すみません、ゆうびんきょくは　どこに________________か。

B: ゆうびんきょくですか？　あそこ________________よ。

A: あ、あれですか。あまり________________ね。

B: ええ、ちいさいですね。

Name ______________________________ Class __________________ Date ____________________

## IV. Describing people, things, and their locations using ～に　～が　あります／います

A. Answer the following questions. If you want to use a proper noun or a foreign word, try to write it in katakana.

■ Example とうきょうに　なにが　ありますか。

じょうとう大学(だいがく)が　あります。

1. ニューヨークに　なにが　ありますか。

______________________________________________

2. ハリウッド (*Hollywood*) に　だれが　いますか。

______________________________________________

3. フロリダに　なにが　ありますか。

______________________________________________

4. ちゅうごくに　なにが　いますか。

______________________________________________

5. パリ (*Paris*) に　どんな　たてものが　ありますか。

______________________________________________

6. ワシントン D.C. に　ゆうめいな　ひとが　いますね。だれが　いますか。

______________________________________________

B: Complete the following dialogue.

**1.** A: シカゴに　どんな　たてものが ________________________。

B: そうですね、たかい　たてもの ________________________。

**2.** A: このへんに　びょういんが ____________________ か。

B: ええ、________________ よ。

A: そうですか。どんな ____________________。

B: りっぱな　たてものですよ。

**3.** A: すみません、このへんに　コンビニ ____________________。

B: ええ、__________________ よ。

A: そうですか、どこ ____________________ か。

B: あそこ ______________________ よ。

 

Name ______________________________ Class __________________ Date ____________________

## V. Using よ and ね

Fill in the blanks with either よ or ね.

■ Example A: やまださんは　学生(がくせい)です＿ね＿。

B: ええ、そうです。

1. A: やまださんの　うちは　とても　きれいです＿＿＿。

   B: ええ、そうですね。

2. A：すみません、いま　なんじですか。

   B：ごじはんです＿＿＿。

   A：そうですか。どうも　ありがとうございます。

3. A：すみません、ぎんこうは　どこに　ありますか。

   B：ぎんこうですか。そこです＿＿＿。

   A：あかい　たてものですか。

   B：いいえ、しろい　たてものです＿＿＿。

   A：ああ、大(おお)きい　たてものです＿＿＿。わかりました。
   ありがとうございます。

4. たなか：きのう　なんじごろ　ばんごはんを　たべましたか。

   スミス：ろくじごろ　たべました＿＿＿。たなかさんは？

   たなか：ぼくは　しちじごろ　たべました＿＿＿。

5. ブラウン：あのう、先生(せんせい)、テストは　げつようびです＿＿＿＿＿。

   先生(せんせい)：いいえ、ブラウンさん、あしたです＿＿＿。

   ブラウン：え？　あしたですか？

   先生(せんせい)：そうですよ。べんきょうして　ください。

Name ______________________ Class ______________ Date ________________

# そうごうれんしゅう **Integration**

Mr. Sato and Mr. Hayashi live in the same dormitory at Joto University. They bumped into each other in front of McDonald's near Shibuya station around 1:30PM. Complete their conversation.

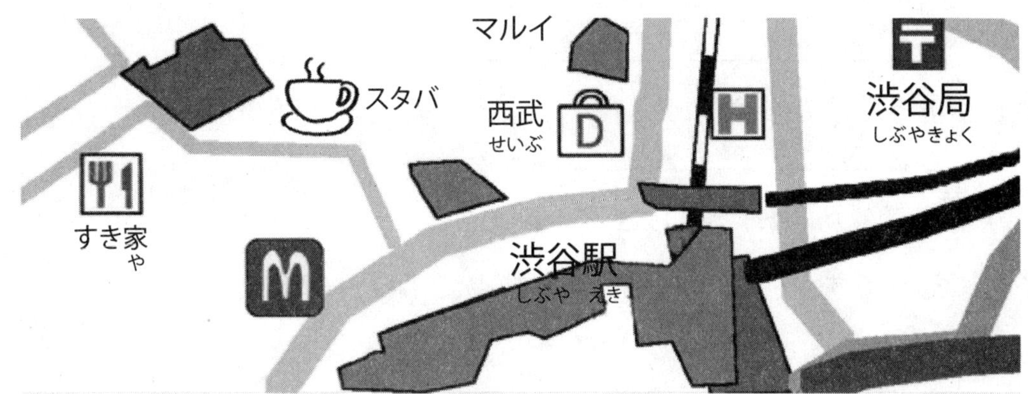


さとう：あ、こんにちは、はやしさん。ひるごはん________________？

はやし：ええ、たべましたよ。さとうさんは？

さとう：ぼくも　すき家(や)で______________________よ。

はやし：え？　すき家(や)って______________________？

さとう：ぎゅうどん (*beef bowl*) の　レストランですよ。

はやし：そうですか。すき家(や)は____________________？

さとう：あれですよ。はやしさんは　これから (*from now*)　なにを　しますか？

はやし：ぼくは　あたらしい　T シャツを　かいたいです (*want to buy*)。

　　　　このへんに　デパートが______________________？

さとう：ええ、西武(せいぶ)デパート_____________________よ。

はやし：西武(せいぶ)デパートは______________________？

さとう：あそこ______________________よ。

はやし：とても　りっぱな　たてものですね。

さとう：そうですね。

はやし：さとうさんは　これから (*from now*) どこ__________________？

さとう：スタバに　いきます。

はやし：スタバで　なに＿＿＿＿＿＿＿＿＿＿＿＿＿＿＿＿？

さとう：コーヒー＿＿＿＿＿＿＿＿＿＿＿＿＿。そして、れきしの　しゅくだい

＿＿＿＿＿＿＿＿＿＿＿＿＿＿＿＿＿。

はやし：そうですか。さとうさん、きょう　なんじごろ　りょう＿＿＿＿＿＿＿＿
＿＿＿＿＿＿＿＿＿＿＿＿＿＿？

さとう：たぶん (*maybe*)　ごじごろ　かえりますよ。

はやし：そうですか、じゃあ　また　あとで (*see you later*)。

Name ______________ Class ______________ Date ______________

# かく　れんしゅう Writing Practice

A. Look at the chart on page a-161 of your textbook and write each **kanji** ten times using the handwritten style.

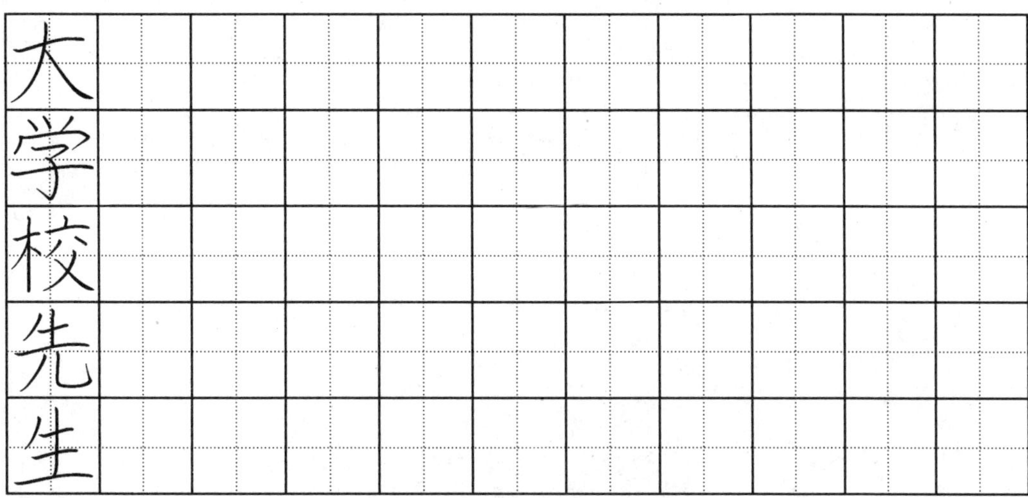


B. Rewrite each sentence using **kanji, hiragana,** and **katakana.**

**1.** わたしの　だいがくは　あまり　おおきくありません。

______________________________

**2.** がっこうは　どこに　ありますか。

______________________________

**3.** あそこに　にほんごの　せんせいが　います。

______________________________

**4.** すみすさんは　がくせいです。

______________________________

Name ______________________ Class ______________ Date ________________

# ラボの　れんしゅう **Lab Activities**

## Part 1: Vocabulary

Please turn to the vocabulary list on pages a-124–a-126 of your textbook and repeat each word or phrase you hear.

Name ______________________ Class ______________ Date ________________

## Part 2: Speaking and Listening Comprehension Activities

### I. Referring to things using これ, それ, あれ, どれ

A. Look at the drawing of a street. You and a friend are at locations A and B in front of the police box and your friend is telling you about the buildings. Listen carefully and circle はい if the statement is true, and いいえ if it is false.

■ You hear: それは　スーパーです。

You circle: はい

**1.** はい　いいえ　**3.** はい　いいえ　**5.** はい　いいえ

**2.** はい　いいえ　**4.** はい　いいえ

B. Listen to each statement **Ms. Kimura makes** about the items pictured. Circle はい if it is true and いいえ if it is false.

■ You hear: これは　にほんごで　かばんと　いいます。

You circle: いいえ

**1.** はい　いいえ　　**3.** はい　いいえ　　**5.** はい　いいえ

**2.** はい　いいえ　　**4.** はい　いいえ

 

Name ______________________ Class ________________ Date ________________

## II. Asking for and giving locations using ～は ～に あります／います and ここ，そこ，あそこ

Look at the drawing of a room. You are at location A and your friend is at location B. Listen carefully to what your friend says and circle the appropriate words from the list.

■ You hear: やまださんは どこに いますか

You circle: （ここ (そこ) あそこ） に（あります (います)）

1. （ここ そこ あそこ）に（あります います）。
2. （ここ そこ あそこ）に（あります います）。
3. （ここ そこ あそこ）に（あります います）。
4. （ここ そこ あそこ）に（あります います）。
5. （ここ そこ あそこ）に（あります います）。

Name ______________________ Class ________________ Date ________________

## III. Describing people and things using adjective + noun, and polite present forms of adjectives

A. First, look at the chart describing various buildings and places. Then listen to each question and circle はい if the answer is true and いいえ if it is false. Stop the audio as necessary.

■ You hear: たなかさんの　アパートは　きれいな　アパートですか。

You circle: はい

| たなかさんの　アパート | きれい　ちいさい |
|---|---|
| 大学(だいがく)の　りょう | ふるい　たかい |
| すずきさんの　うち | あたらしい　ちいさい |
| としょかん | りっぱ　ちゃいろい |
| じょうとう大学(だいがく) | 大(おお)きい　ゆうめい　いい |

**1.** はい　いいえ　　**3.** はい　いいえ　　**5.** はい　いいえ

**2.** はい　いいえ　　**4.** はい　いいえ　　**6.** はい　いいえ

B. Look at the following illustrations and make a statement about each, using adjective + noun. You will hear the correct answer. Then stop the audio and write it.

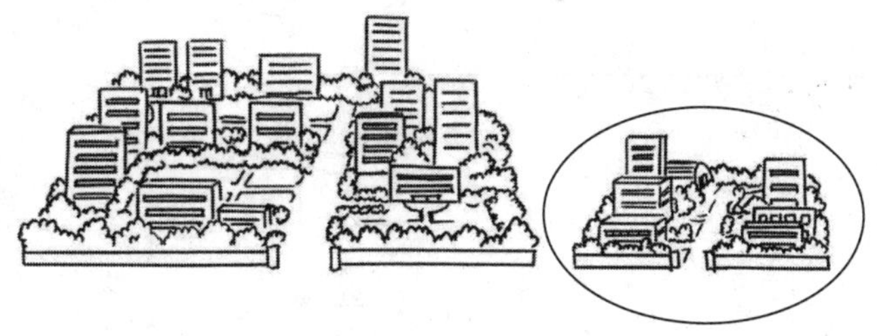

■ You say: わたしの　大学(だいがく)は　ちいさい　大学(だいがく)です

You hear: わたしの　大学(だいがく)は　ちいさい　大学(だいがく)です。

You write: わたしの　大学(だいがく)は　ちいさい　大学(だいがく)です。

1. ______________________________

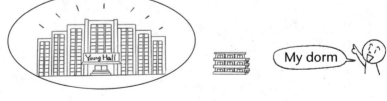

My apartment

2. ______________________________

RED

My bag

3. ______________________________

4. ______________________________

BANK

5. ______________________________

Young Hall

My dorm

6. ______________________________

 

Name ______________________ Class ________________ Date ________________

C. Mr. Li is talking about his university. Listen and write the dictionary form of each adjective that describes it. Then decide whether the statement is affirmative or negative.

■ You hear: わたしの　大学(だいがく)は　とても　ふるいです。

You write: 大学(だいがく) ふるい (affirmative negative) [affirmative circled]

1. 大学(だいがく) ______________________ (affirmative negative)

2. ラボ ______________________ (affirmative negative)

3. りょう ______________________ (affirmative negative)

4. としょかん ______________________ (affirmative negative)

5. ほんや ______________________ (affirmative negative)

6. ゆうびんきょくの　たてもの ______________ (affirmative negative)

D. Listen and answer the questions according to the cues you hear. Then repeat the correct answer after the speaker.

■ You hear: 大学(だいがく)の　たてものは　大(おお)きいですか。/ いいえ

You say: いいえ、大(おお)きくありません。 or 大(おお)きくないです。

You hear: いいえ、大(おお)きくありません。 or 大(おお)きくないです。

You hear: 大学(だいがく)の　たてものは　大(おお)きいですか。/ ええ　とても

You say: ええ、とても　大(おお)きいです。

You hear: ええ、とても　大(おお)きいです。

Name ______________________ Class ________________ Date ________________

## IV. Describing people, things, and their locations using 〜に 〜が ありますノいます

Answer each of the following questions orally. Then write the answer. Stop the audio as necessary.

■ You hear: 大学に(だいがく) なにが ありますか。

You say : 大きい(おお) としょかんが あります。

You write: 大きい(おお) としょかんが あります。

1. ____________________________________________

2. ____________________________________________

3. ____________________________________________

4. ____________________________________________

5. ____________________________________________

6. ____________________________________________

Name ______________________ Class ______________ Date ________________

## V. Using よ and ね

A. Answer the following questions using よ. Then, stop the audio and write your answer.

■ You hear: 学生(がくせい)ですか。

You say: ええ、そうですよ。

You write: ええ、そうですよ。

1. ______________________________

2. ______________________________

3. ______________________________

4. ______________________________

5. ______________________________

6. ______________________________

B. Comfirm the questions you hear with ね. If ね cannot be used, say "impossible." Then, stop the audio and write your answer. Follow the model.

■ You hear: 学生(がくせい)ですか。

You say : 学生(がくせい)ですね。

You hear: 学生(がくせい)ですね。

You write: 学生(がくせい)ですね。

You hear: あれは　なんですか。

You say: impossible

You hear: impossible

You write: impossible

1. ______________________________

2. ______________________________

3. ______________________________

4. ______________________________

5. ______________________________

6. ______________________________

 

Name ______________________ Class ______________ Date ______________

## Part 3: Dict-a-Conversation

You, Smith, are talking with your Japanese friend Mr. Kimura. You are asking him about various buildings around town.

スミス：(*pointing at a nearby building*) ______________________________

きむら：______________________________

スミス：______________________________

きむら：______________________________

スミス：______________________________

きむら：______________________________

スミス：______________________________

Name ______________________ Class ______________ Date ________________

# Chapter 5
# だいごか

# Japanese Homes

# 日本(にほん)の　うち

## Workbook Activities

### たんごの　れんしゅう　Vocabulary Practice

Answer the following questions in Japanese.

**1.** 今日(きょう)　学食(がくしょく)へ　いきましたか。

_______________________________________________

**2.** ～さん (*you*) の　へやに　コンピュータが　ありますか。どんな
コンピュータですか。

_______________________________________________

**3.** ～さんは　じてんしゃが　ありますか。

_______________________________________________

**4.** 大学の　たいいくかんは、どこに　ありますか。きれいな　たてものですか。

_______________________________________________

**5.** 日本語(にほんご)の　きょうしつは　くらいですか。

_______________________________________________

**6.** ～さんの　りょう／アパート／うちは、しずかですか。

_______________________________________________

Name ______________________ Class ________________ Date __________________

## I. Referring to people, places, and things using この，その，あの，どの

Look at the drawing of a room. Imagine that Ms. Ueda is sitting on the bed and Ms. Kimura is in front of the bookshelf. Complete the following conversation using この, その, あの, どの.

きむら：上田(うえだ)さん、＿＿この＿＿へやは　上田(うえだ)さんの　へやですか。

上田(うえだ)：　ええ、そうです。

きむら：とても　あかるいですね。あのう、＿＿＿＿＿いぬは　上田(うえだ)さんの　いぬですか。

上田(うえだ)：　ええ、そうです。なまえは　チビタンです。

きむら：かわいい (*cute*) ですね。＿＿＿＿＿ねこも　上田(うえだ)さんの　ねこですか。

上田(うえだ)：　え？＿＿＿＿＿ねこですか。

きむら：(*pointing out the window*) ＿＿＿＿＿ねこですよ。

上田(うえだ)：　ああ、＿＿＿＿＿ねこは　となり (*neighbor*) の　ねこです。

きむら：そうですか。ところで (*by the way*)、上田(うえだ)さん。＿＿＿＿＿とけいは　とても　きれいですね。

上田(うえだ)：　ええ。あたらしい　とけいですよ。

Name ______________________ Class ______________ Date ______________

## II. Using location nouns: 中(なか), そと, となり, よこ, ちかく, うしろ, まえ, 上(うえ), 下(した), みぎ, ひだり

A. Look at the drawing of Mr. Suzuki's room. Complete the following description, by putting the correct location nouns in parentheses and fill in the blanks with the most appropriate words. Use your right and left as you look at the room.

すずきさんの　へやの（　　　　）に　あたらしい　ベッドが　あります。ベッドの（　　　　）に　きれいな　えが　あります。そして、テレビの（　　　　）に　キャビネット (*cabinet*) が　あります。キャビネットの（　　　　）には　日本(にほん)の　えいがの　DVDが　あります。すずきさんは　しゅうまつ　よく　DVDを ______________。つくえの（　　　　）に　本(ほん)だなが　あります。本(ほん)だなの（　　　　）に　すずきさんの　ごりょうしん (*parents*) の　しゃしんが　あります。本(ほん)だなの（　　　　）には　たくさん (*many*) 本(ほん)が　あります。すずきさんは　ときどき　そとの　きの（　　　　）で　本(ほん)を ______________。

B. Look at the drawing in Activity A, and describe the following objects using location nouns.

■ Example　おしいれ　　へやの　みぎに　おしいれが　あります。

1. ドア ________________

2. とけい ________________

3. いぬ ________________

4. コンピュータ ________________

5. ふとん ________________

C. Look at the street map. You (A) are a police officer standing in front of the police box. People come up to ask you about different places in the neighborhood. Answer their questions using location nouns.

Name ______________________ Class ________________ Date ________________

**1.** A: きっさてんは　どこに　ありますか。

B: ________________________________________

**2.** A: びょういんの　まえに　なにが　ありますか。

B: ________________________________________

**3.** A: 本(ほん)やの　となりの　たてものは、なんですか。

B: ________________________________________

**4.** A: 本(ほん)やの　まえに　なにが　ありますか。

B: ________________________________________

**5.** A: こうえんの　まえの　たてものは、なんですか。

B: ________________________________________

**6.** A: りょうは　どの　たてものですか。

B: ________________________________________

## III. Referring to things mentioned immediately before, using noun/adjective + の (pronoun)

A. Write appropriate statements using adjective + の. Refer to the chart below for information on various university facilities.

| 学生かいかん | ラボ | としょかん | たいいくかん |
|---|---|---|---|
| 大きい<br>きれい | しずか<br>せまい | あたらしい<br>あかるい | ふるい<br>りっぱ |

■ Example　大きい　　大きいのは　がくせいかいかんです。

1. せまい ________________________________________
2. きれい ________________________________________
3. りっぱ ________________________________________
4. あかるい ________________________________________
5. しずか ________________________________________

B. Fill in the blanks with the appropriate expressions, using adjective/noun + の.

| | 山田(やまだ) | スミス | キム | リン |
|---|---|---|---|---|
| じしょ | 小(ちい)さい | きれい | あたらしい | 小(ちい)さい |
| ノート | あかい | しろい | あおい | くろい |
| きょうかしょ | きれい | ふるい | あたらしい | あたらしい |

■ Example くろい　ノートは　リンさんの　です。

**1.** しろい　ノートは________________です。　あかいのは__________________です。

**2.** あたらしい　じしょは_______________です。______________は　スミスさんのです。

**3.** きれいな　きょうかしょは______________です。ふるいのは__________________です。

**4.** キムさんの　きょうかしょは　あたらしいです。______________________も　あたらしいです。

**5.** 山田(やまだ)さんの　ノートは　あかいです。　でも (*but*)、_____________は　あおいです。

**6.** 山田(やまだ)さんの　じしょは　小(ちい)さい　じしょです。__________________も　小(ちい)さいです。

 

Name ______________________________ Class __________________ Date ___________________

## V. More about the topic marker は and the similarity marker も (double particles and は vs. が )

A. Complete each of the following sentences by filling in the blanks with the correct particle(s) to mark each **topic**.

■ Example 昨日(きのう)　本(ほん)やに　いきました。

その　本(ほん)や<u>には</u>　日本語(にほんご)の　じしょが　ありました。

**1.** あそこに　山田(やまだ)さんが　います。山田(やまだ)さん _____　とうきょうから　きました。

**2.** 今日(きょう)の　ごご　大学の　ちかくの　カフェで　コーヒーを　のみます。

その　カフェ _______　とても　きれいです。

**3.** わたしの　大学は　じょうとう大学です。

大学 ________　大きい　としょかんが　あります。

**4.** おととい　日本(にほん)の　レストランに　いきました。

その　レストラン _______　すしを　たべました。

**5.** いま　くじです。くじ ________　いい　テレビばんぐみ (*program*) が　あります。

B. Fill in the blanks of the following conversational exchanges with the particle も or a double particle (*X* も).

**1.** A: わたしは　まいあさ　コーヒーを　のみます。

B: そうですか。オレンジジュース _____ のみますか。

A: ええ、のみますよ。

**2.** A: たいてい　どこで　べんきょうしますか。

B: そうですね、よく　としょかんで　します。

A: へや ________ しますか。

B: ええ、しますよ。

3. A: 日本語(にほんご)の　じゅぎょうは、もくようびに　ありますか。

　B: ええ、きんようび ________ ありますよ。

C. Fill in the blanks of the following conversational exchanges with は, が or も.

1. A: あのう、すみません。 ゆうびんきょく________どこに　ありますか。

　B: ゆうびんきょくですか。　そこですよ。

　A: そうですか。どうも　ありがとう　ございます。

2. A: リーさん________どの　人(ひと)ですか。

　B: あの　人(ひと)です。

3. 田中(たなか): 　山田(やまだ)さんの　けしゴム _____どれですか。

　山田(やまだ): 　これです。

　田中(たなか): 　そうですか。あれ______ 山田(やまだ)さんのですか。

　山田(やまだ): 　いいえ、 スミスさんのです。

4. A: どの　たてもの________ えきですか。

　B: あれ ______ えきですよ。

　A: 大きいですね。　じゃあ、こうばん________ どれですか。

　B: そこに　小(ちい)さい　たてもの________ありますね。　それですよ。

5. A: そこに　いぬ________いますよ。

　B: えっ。どこですか。

　A: そこに　あかい　かばん______ありますね。　いぬ______その　かばんの
　うしろに　います。

6. A: だれ______昨日(きのう)の　パーティに　いきましたか。

　B: すずきさん________いきました。

 

Name ______________________ Class ______________ Date ________________

# かく　れんしゅう Writing Practice

A. Look at the chart on page a-204 of your textbook and write each **kanji** ten times using the handwritten style.

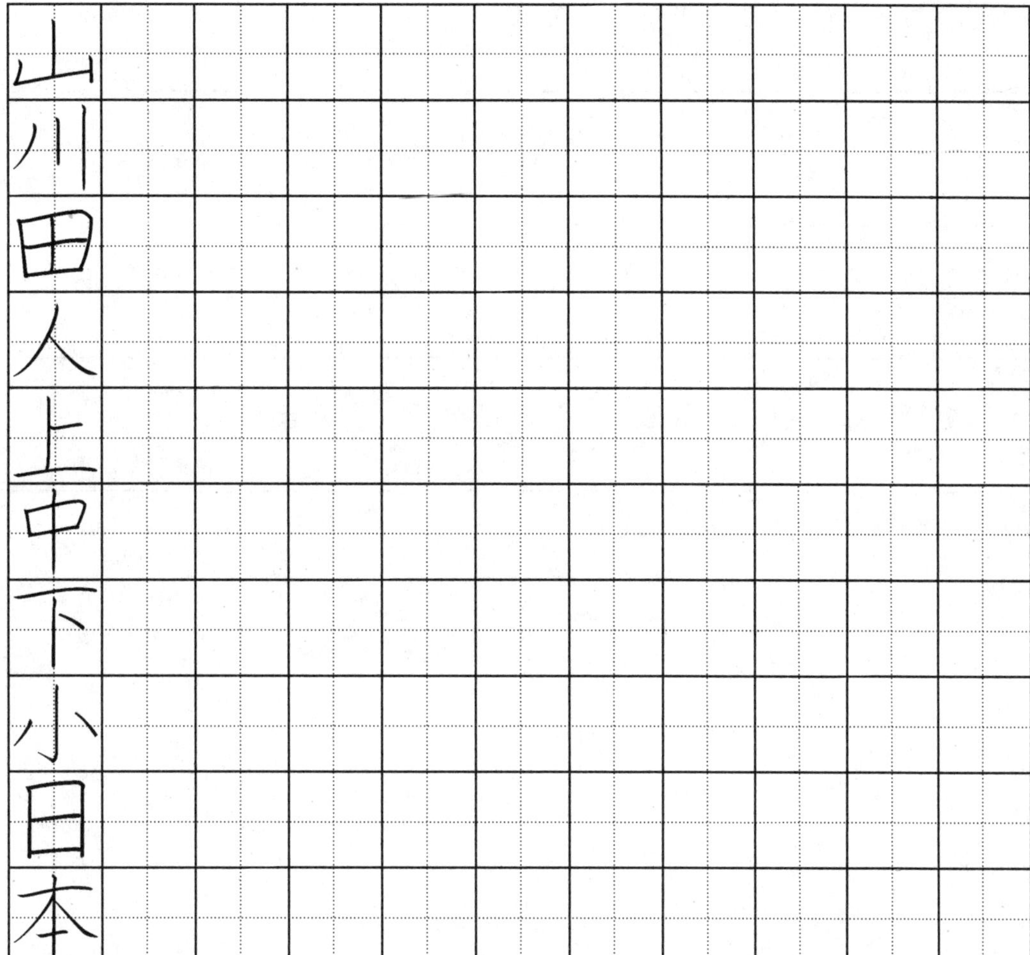

B. Rewrite each sentence using **kanji, hiragana,** and **katakana.**

**1.** やまだせんせいは　にほんじんです。

**2.** やまかわさんは　だいがくせいです。

**3.** たなかさんの　あぱーとは　ちいさいです。

**4.** つくえの　うえに　おおかわさんの　にほんごの　のーとが　あります。

**5.** ほんやの　なかの　かふぇで　こーひーを　のみました。

Name ______________________ Class ______________ Date ________________

# ラボの　れんしゅう　Lab Activities

## Part 1: Vocabulary

Please turn to the vocabulary list on pages a-166–a-168 of your textbook and repeat each word or phrase you hear.

## Part 2: Speaking and Listening Comprehension Activities

### I. Referring to people, places, and things using この, その, あの, どの

Look at the drawing of a bedroom. You are sitting on the sofa and your friend is in front of the cabinet. Your friend is commenting on different objects in the room. Circle はい if the object he/she refers to is in the correct location with respect to where you and your friend are.

■ You hear: この　へやは　きれいですね。

You circle: (はい) いいえ　because both of you are in the room.

1. はい　いいえ　　3. はい　いいえ　　5. はい　いいえ

2. はい　いいえ　　4. はい　いいえ

Name ______________________ Class ______________ Date ______________

## II. Using location nouns: 中(なか), そと, となり, よこ, ちかく, うしろ, まえ, 上(うえ), 下(した), みぎ, ひだり

A. Look at the drawing of a bedroom. Listen to each conversational exchange and circle はい if it is correct and いいえ if it is incorrect.

■ You hear: A: ドアの　よこに　なにが　ありますか。

B: おしいれが　あります。

You circle: はい　(いいえ)　because the closet is not next to the door.

1. はい　いいえ　　3. はい　いいえ　　5. はい　いいえ

2. はい　いいえ　　4. はい　いいえ　　6. はい　いいえ

B. Look at the drawing of the classroom. Answer each of the following questions. You will then hear the correct answer. Write each answer.

■ You hear: こくばんは　どこに　ありますか。

You say: 先生の　うしろに　あります。

You hear: 先生の　うしろに　あります。

You write: <u>先生の　うしろに　あります。</u>

1. ______________________________

2. ______________________________

3. ______________________________

4. ______________________________

5. ______________________________

6. ______________________________

 

Name ______________________ Class ______________ Date ______________

## III. Referring to things mentioned immediately before, using noun/ adjective + の (pronoun)

Listen for the adjective/noun + の in each conversational exchange. Write the expression with the adjective/nouns + の (pronoun). Also write what の refers to in that phrase. Stop the audio as necessary.

■ You hear: A: この　えんぴつは　すずきさんの　えんぴつですか。

B: いいえ。山田(やまだ)さんのです。

You write: 山田(やまだ)さんの and えんぴつ

| | Adjective/noun ＋ の | what の refers to |
|---|---|---|
| 1 | | |
| 2 | | |
| 3 | | |
| 4 | | |
| 5 | | |

Name ______________________ Class ______________ Date ________________

## IV. Expressing distance and duration using the particles から, まで and で and the suffix ～ぐらい／くらい

Listen to the following conversations and answer each question in writing.

■ You hear: A: なんじに　大学に　きますか。

B: たいてい　くじに　きます。　でも　今日(きょう)は　はちじに　きました。

A: ああ、そうですか。

You see: この人(ひと)は　今日(きょう)　なんじに　大学に　きましたか。

You write: はちじに　きました。

**1.** この人(ひと)は　昨日(きのう)　どのぐらい　テレビを　みましたか。

______________________________________________

**2.** この人(ひと)は　今日(きょう)、じてんしゃで　大学に　きましたか。

______________________________________________

**3.** テストは　なんじから　なんじまで　ありますか。

______________________________________________

**4.** うちから　学校まで　あるいて　どのぐらい　かかりますか。

______________________________________________

Name ______________________ Class ______________ Date ______________

## V. More about the topic marker は and the similarity marker も (double particles and は vs. が )

A. After listening to each conversational exchange, read the first statement, then write a second statement that reflects what you heard. Use は or も in your statements.

■ You hear: A: きのう　日本語(にほんご)の　べんきょうを　しましたか。

B: ええ。

A: こんばんも　しますか。

B: ええ、こんばんも　しますよ。

You see: きのう　日本語(にほんご)の　べんきょうを　しました。______________

You write: こんばんも　します。

1. この　たてものは　としょかんです。______________________

2. しゅうまつ、テレビを　みました。______________________

3. げつようびに　たいいくかんに　いきます。______________________

4. うちで　ひるごはんを　たべます。______________________

B. You will hear two short phrases. Combine them into a question using either は or が. You will then hear the correct question. Then write each question.

■ You hear: だれ　先生ですか。

You say: だれが　先生ですか。

You hear: だれが　先生ですか。

You write: だれが　先生ですか。

1. ______________________________

2. ______________________________

3. ______________________________

4. ______________________________

5. ______________________________

6. ______________________________

7. ______________________________

8. ______________________________

 

Name ______________ Class ______________ Date ______________

## Part 3: Dict-a-Conversation

You (Smith) are telling your friend, Mr. Kimura, about your room.

きむら：______________________________

スミス：______________________________

きむら：______________________________

スミス：______________________________

きむら：______________________________

スミス：______________________________

きむら：______________________________

スミス：______________________________

きむら：______________________________

スミス：______________________________

Name ______________________ Class ______________ Date ______________

# Chapter 6
# だいろっか
# Leisure Time
# 休(やす)みの　日

---

## Workbook Activities

### たんごの　れんしゅう　Vocabulary Practice

Answer the following questions in Japanese.

1. 毎週(まいしゅう)、せんたくを　しますか。

_______________________________________________

2. 毎(まい)日、メールを　かきますか。

_______________________________________________

3. どんな　おんがくを　よく　ききますか。

_______________________________________________

4. 昨日(きのう)、ともだちに　あいましたか。どこで　あいましたか。

_______________________________________________

5. 昨日(きのう)、でんわを　かけましたか。

_______________________________________________

6. 今週(こんしゅう)は　いそがしいですか。

_______________________________________________

7. 日本語(にほんご)の　しゅくだいは　むずかしいですか。

_______________________________________________

8. 今(いま)、おもしろい　えいがが　ありますか。

_______________________________________________

Name ______________________ Class ______________ Date ________________

## II. Commenting about the past, using polite past adjectives and the copula verb です

A. Complete each of the following chart.

| Dictionary Form | Polite Past Tense Affirmative | Polite Past Tense Negative |
|---|---|---|
| 大きい | 大きかったです | 大きくありませんでした<br>大きくなかったです |
| たいへん | | |
| たのしい | | |
| だいじょうぶ | | |
| むずかしい | | |
| いい | | |
| ひま | | |
| おもしろい | | |
| きれい | | |
| 日本人 | | |

B. Complete each of the following sentences by filling in the parentheses with the correct adjective forms. You also need to supply the appropriate word or phrase for each blank.

■ Example A: 先週の 土曜日の パーティに いきましたか。
せんしゅう どようび

B: ええ、いきましたよ。とても （にぎやかでした）。
にぎやか

1. A: おとといの テストは （ ）か。
むずかしい

B: いいえ、あまり（ ）。

2. A: きのう 日本語の しゅくだいを ＿＿＿＿＿＿＿＿か。
にほんご

B: ええ、＿＿＿＿＿＿＿＿。

A: （ ）か。
たいへん

B: いいえ、あまり（ ）。

3. A: 昨日は（ ）か。
きのう
いそがしい

B: ええ、とても（ ）よ。たくさん しごとを＿＿＿＿＿＿＿＿。

4. A: 先週の 金曜日に 何を ＿＿＿＿＿＿＿＿か。
せんしゅう きんようび なに

B: 大学で 日本の えいがを ＿＿＿＿＿＿＿＿。

A: そうですか。えいがは＿＿＿＿＿＿＿＿か。

B: とても（ ）。
いい

 

Name ______________________ Class ______________ Date ______________

## V. Extending an invitation using ませんか

A. Complete the following invitations by filling in the correct particle in parentheses and the correct phrase for each blank.

**1.** レストラン(　　)　すし(　　)　______________________。

**2.** こうえん(　　)　さんぽ(　　)　______________________。

**3.** 明日(あした)　いっしょ(　　)　プール(　　)　______________________。

**4.** 金曜日(きんようび)(　　)日本(　　)　アニメ(　　)　______________________。

**5.** 今晩(こんばん)　カフェ(　　)　コーヒー(　　)　のみ(　　)______________________。

B. Complete the following conversations by writing the appropriate phrases in the blanks.

**1.** A: 今度(こんど)の　休(やす)みは　いそがしいですか。

B: いいえ、______________________。

A: そうですか。じゃあ、デパートに　かいもの ______________________。

B: ええ、______________________。

**2.** A: 今晩(こんばん)、学生かいかんで　日本語(にほんご)______________________。

B: 今晩(こんばん)ですか？　すみません、今晩(こんばん)は ちょっと ______________________。

A: そうですか、ざんねんですね。

Name ______________________ Class ________________ Date ________________

# そうごうれんしゅう Integration

Ms. Ueda and Mr. Li met on campus on Monday. Complete their conversation by filling in the blanks.

上田： あ、リーさん、おはようございます。

リー： おはようございます。上田さん、週末(しゅうまつ) ______________________？

上田： とても　いそがしかったですよ。たくさん　しゅくだいが __________、
たいへんでした。リーさんは？

リー： 私は　とても　たのしかったです。ともだちと　えいが __________、
レストランに　ばんごはん ______________________。

上田： そうですか。どの　レストランに ______________________？

リー： 日本りょうりの　レストランに __________________よ。なまえは
ななくさです。すしと　てんぷら __________、日本の　ビール
__________________。

上田： その　レストランは ______________________________？

リー： デパートの　ちかくに ______________。あたらし ________、
きれい ________ レストランですよ。

上田： そうですか、いいですね。

リー： 上田さん、今度(こんど)　いっしょに　ななくさに ______________________？

上田： ええ、ぜひ。

リー： 今度(こんど)の　土曜日(どようび)は　いそがしいですか？

上田： いいえ、______________________。

リー： じゃあ、土曜日(どようび)の　ごご、でんわを　して __________________か？

上田： わかりました。じゃあ、でんわを　かけますね。

Name ______________________ Class ______________ Date ________________

# かく　れんしゅう Writing Practice

A. Look at the chart on pages a-243–a-244 of your textbook and write each **kanji** ten times using the handwritten style.

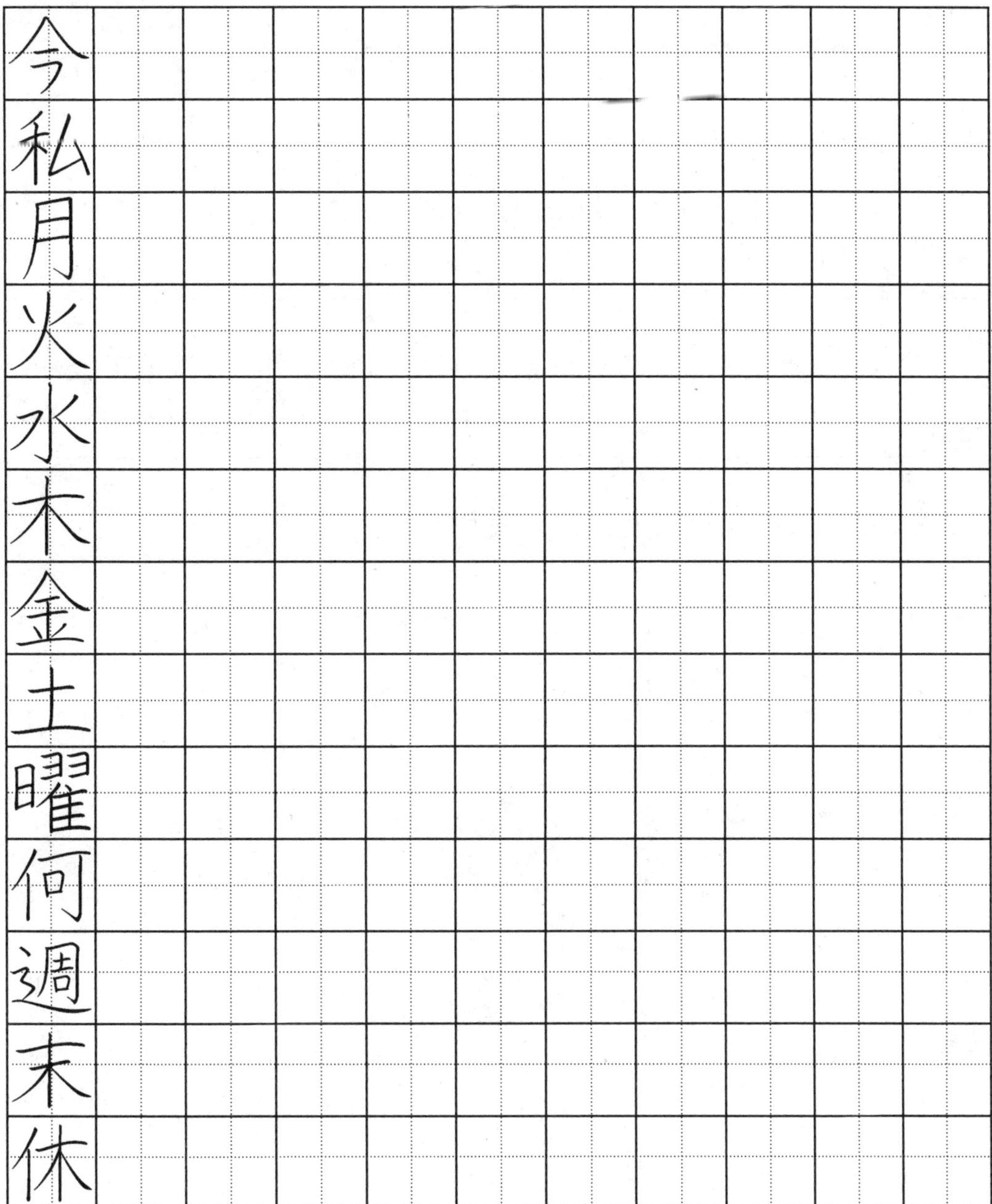

B. Rewrite each sentence using the **kanji** you have learned.

**1.** しゅうまつ、なにを　しましたか。

________________________________________

**2.** いま　かばんの　なかに　なにが　ありますか。

________________________________________

**3.** わたしは　きんようびに　おおかわせんせいに　あいます。

________________________________________

**4.** やまださんは　せんしゅうの　やすみに　にほんから　きました。

________________________________________

**5.** なんようびに　がっこうに　いきますか。

________________________________________

Name ______________________ Class ______________ Date ________________

# ラボの　れんしゅう **Lab Activities**

## Part 1: Vocabulary

Please turn to the vocabulary list on pages a-210–a-212 of your textbook and repeat each word or phrase you hear.

## Part 2: Speaking and Listening Comprehension Activities

### I. Using the particles と and に

A. Listen to each of the following incomplete sentences and say a complete sentence, using the correct particle. You will then hear the correct sentence.

■ You hear: 先生 / メール / かきます

You say: 先生に　メールを　かきます。

You hear: 先生に　メールを　かきます。

You repeat: 先生に　メールを　かきます。

B. Listen to the following conversations. Then answer each question in writing.

■ You hear: A: 昨日(きのう)　おもしろい　えいがを　みましたよ。

B: そうですか。だれと　みましたか。

A: キムさんと　みました。

B: ああ、そうですか。

You see: この人は　だれと　えいがを　みましたか。

________________________みました。

You write: キムさんと　みました。

1. この人は　だれに　よく　てがみを　かきますか。

________________________かきます。

2. この人は　昨日(きのう)　だれと　レストランに　いきましたか。

________________________いきました。

3. この人は　何曜日(なんようび)に　たいいくかんに　いきますか。

________________________いきます。

C. Listen to each of the following conversations and write in English each destination and purpose. Stop the audio as necessary.

■ You hear: A: スミスさん、おでかけですか。

B: ええ、ちょっと　えきの　まえの　デパートまで。

A: おかいものですか。

B: ええ、そうです。

Your write: Destination: department store　Purpose: to go shopping

| | Destination | Purpose |
|---|---|---|
| 1. | ________________ | ________________ |
| 2. | ________________ | ________________ |
| 3. | ________________ | ________________ |
| 4. | ________________ | ________________ |

Name ______________________________ Class ___________________ Date ____________________

## II. Commenting about the past, using polite past adjectives and the copula verb です

A. Listen to seven questions and cues. Answer each question, using the cues. You will then hear the correct answer.

■ You hear: えいがは　どうでしたか。/ あまり / おもしろい

You say: あまり　おもしろくありませんでした。

You hear: あまり　おもしろくありませんでした。

You repeat: あまり　おもしろくありませんでした。

B. Listen to the following conversations. After each conversation, stop the audio and fill in the blank with the appropriate past adjective to complete each statement about the conversation.

■ You hear: A: 昨日(きのう)　べんきょうしましたか。

B: いいえ、 ぜんぜん　しませんでしたよ。山田さんは？

A: ぼくは　しましたよ。日本語(にほんご)の　しゅくだいは　大変(たいへん)でしたからね。

You see: 日本語(にほんご)の　しゅくだいは ______________________

You write: 日本語(にほんご)の　しゅくだいは たいへんでした。

1. テストは　あまり ______________________________

2. えいがは　とても ______________________________

3. へやは　あまり ______________________________

4. シカゴの　ダウンタウンは　とても ______________________

Name ______________________ Class ______________ Date ______________

## III. Connecting verb and adjective phrases and sentences using the て-form of verbs; making requests using the て-form

A. You will hear the ～ます form of twelve verbs. Change each verb to its て-form and add 下さい. You will then hear the correct response. Repeat each response.

■ You hear: みます。

You say: みて下さい。

You hear: みて下さい。

You repeat: みて下さい。

B. You will now hear the ～ます form of twelve more verbs. Change each verb to its て- form and くれませんか. You will then hear the correct response. Repeat each response.

■ You hear: みます。

You say: みてくれませんか。

You hear: みてくれませんか。

You repeat: みてくれませんか。

C. Listen to each of the following conversations. After each conversation, look at the statement and choose the correct answer.

■ You hear: A: キムさん、日本語(にほんご)で はなして下さい。

B: はい、どうもすみません

You see and choose: Mr. Kim was asked: (to speak in Japanese) to write in Japanese

1. Mr. Kim was asked: to look at the textbook to read the textbook

2. Mr. Kim was asked: to come to the teacher to listen to the teacher

3. Mr. Kim was asked: to come to the teacher to listen to the teacher

Name ______________________ Class ________________ Date ________________

## IV. Connecting phrases, using the て-forms of verbs and adjectives

A. Listen to each of the following pairs of short sentences. Say a statement that combines the short sentences, using the て- form of the first verb. You will then hear the correct statement. Repeat and then write each statement.

■ You hear: としょかんに　いきます。/ べんきょうします。

You say: としょかんに　いって、　べんきょうします。

You hear: としょかんに　いって、　べんきょうします。

You repeat and write: としょかんに　いって、　べんきょうします。

1. ______________________________

2. ______________________________

3. ______________________________

4. ______________________________

5. ______________________________

B. Listen to each of the following pairs of short sentences. Say a statement that combines the short sentences, using the て- form of adjectives/copula verb. You will then hear the correct statement. Repeat and then write each statement.

■ You hear: 大きいです。/ きれいです。

You say: 大きくて、　きれいです。

You hear: 大きくて、　きれいです。

You repeat and write: 大きくて、　きれいです。

1. ______________________________

2. ______________________________

3. ______________________________

4. ______________________________

5. ______________________________

Name ______________________ Class ______________ Date ______________

## V. Extending an invitation using ませんか

A. Listen to each of the following dialogues. After each dialogue, write the activity mentioned in the dialogue. If the person accepts the invitation, circle はい; if the person refuses, circle いいえ.

■ You hear: A: 明日(あした)、えいがを　みに　いきませんか。

B: ええ、ぜひ。

You see: ______________ はい　いいえ

You write: えいがを　みに　いきます。 and circle はい

1. ______________________________ はい　いいえ

2. ______________________________ はい　いいえ

3. ______________________________ はい　いいえ

4. ______________________________ はい　いいえ

B. Listen to each of the following conversations. After each conversation, write a sentence paraphrasing it. Make sure you include the destination and purpose using ～に.

■ You hear: A: 山田さん、週末(しゅうまつ)に　えいがを　みませんか。

B: いいですね。どんな　えいがですか。

A: みやざきの　えいがです。

B: ええ、ぜひ　いきます。私は　みやざきの　ファン (*fan*) ですから。どこで　ありますか。

A: ええと、あっ、ぎんざですよ。

You see: この人は ______________________

You write: この人は　ぎんざに　（みやざきの）えいがを　みに　いきます。

1. この人は ______________________________

2. この人は ______________________________

3. この人は ______________________________

4. この人は ______________________________

Name ______________________ Class ______________ Date ________________

## Part 3: Dict-a-Conversation

You (Smith) are talking with your classmate, Mr. Kimura, who has a part-time job. You are asking questions.

スミス：________________________________________

きむら：________________________________________

スミス：________________________________________

きむら：________________________________________

スミス：________________________________________

きむら：________________________________________

スミス：________________________________________

きむら：________________________________________

スミス：________________________________________

きむら：________________________________________